The Executive Guide
To Call Center Metrics

By James C. Abbott

Robert
Houston
Smith
Publishers

Robert Houston Smith Publishers
PO Box 25156
Greenville, SC 29616
864-627-1278 (telephone)
864-297-8624 (facsimile)
www.RHSPublishers.com
books@RHSPublishers.com

ISBN: 1-887355-08-1

Second Printing

© 2004 by Abbott Associates Incorporated

Printed in the United States of America

Dedication:

For my mother, Alice Abbott, and my grandmothers Beulah Abbott and Blanche D Smith. The strength and grace of these "steel magnolias" profoundly influenced me. I owe them a great deal.

Table of Contents

Introduction 1

Chapter One: Having It All 14

Chapter Two: Call Center Metrics 24

Chapter Three: Monitoring Metrics 43

Chapter Four: Metric Dashboard 61

Chapter Five: Reading the Tactical View 79

Chapter Six: Tactical Use of Metrics 91

Chapter Seven: Strategic Terms 109

Chapter Eight: Strategic View 123

Chapter Nine: Using the Strategic View 143

Chapter Ten: Strategic Decisions Using Metrics .. 165

Chapter Eleven: Benefits of Effective Metrics ... 176

Index 188

Introduction |

What is a Call Center?

The dictionary defines the word **call** as *to get or try to get into communication by telephone*. This definition has served us well for decades. In recent years a somewhat broader definition is required. Broadening to the word "contact" might provide clearer understanding. A **contact** is *a person serving as a go-between, messenger, connection, or source of special information* and it does not restrict the mode to just telephones. The current call center communicates through many modes starting with our old reliable telephone and extending to fax, e-mail, standard mail, Web sites, and so on. In this book when we use the term *call* we are talking about all methods of communication.

A **center** is defined as *a point, area, person, or thing that is most important or pivotal in relation to an indicated activity, interest, or condition or a source from which something originates or a group having a common function or a facility providing a place for a particular activity or service.*

Thus a **call center** is a *group having a common function or a facility providing a place for a particular activity or service serving as a go-between, messenger, connection, or source of special information.*

What Kinds of Businesses Use Call Centers Today?

Service, manufacturing, and the public sector all have call centers. Most don't realize it because they use a different name and tragically miss many techniques that would provide them huge benefits.

Service

The service industry is comprised of many arenas. Insurance, utilities, IT or software, sales, hospitals, telecommunications, and banking is a list of just a few. Let's take some of these industries and list their call centers and how they are referred to.

Insurance businesses provide a means of guaranteeing protection from losses like theft, fire, accident, illness, etc. Insurance companies have call centers under the name of customer care or service centers, claims centers, processing centers, crisis centers, or disaster management centers.

Introduction

Utility companies provide services like electricity, power, sewage, water, and so on. Utility companies have call centers under the name of billing centers or maintenance. The maintenance call center will take care of any outages, failures or poor quality.

Software companies build the programs to run the computers that we depend on so much. Software companies must have call centers that support the software. These are called software support centers. Centers that resolve problems are called problem resolution centers.

Companies that sell through bricks and mortar, e-commerce, or wholesale must have call centers. These call centers do order taking, billing, and customer service.

The health care and medical industry diagnose and treat diseases, treat us after accidents, and help prevent disease. Their call centers are the waiting rooms of a medical practice, the emergency rooms of a hospital, and the hospital's facility maintenance.

The telecommunications industry provides voice and data communication in many forms such as cell phones, phone lines, and Internet service. They use call centers for product hookup, connection, service problems, and maintenance. Their call centers are typically called customer care centers or maintenance service centers.

The banking industry allows us to hold, manage, and transfer our money. Their call centers are referred to as processing centers, customer service, or simply your local branch office.

Public Sector

Federal, state, and local government agencies provide services to our citizens. Agencies like the Veterans Administration, Internal Revenue Service, FEMA, and Department of Defense, to name just a few, must provide information to their constituency. These are typically referred to as customer service centers, crisis and disaster management centers, or hot lines.

Local governments have a 911 help desk to manage and dispatch all kinds of services in a crisis. A help desk is another name for a call center.

Manufacturing

Just about every manufacturing business has call centers doing the facility maintenance, dealing with customer complaints, and providing customer service.

Another area that is huge in manufacturing is the information technology group who manage user setup, software support, and problem resolution. These call centers are typically referred to as help desks.

The chemical and pharmaceuticals industries must have the ability to explain their products. They must also be able to assist when their sometimes-poisonous products are misused. These call centers are typically referred to as customer hot lines.

Manufacturing has built operational techniques, from simple to complex, that are usable no matter what the business. This knowledge has allowed them huge efficiencies and will also be essential as call centers become more complex. These dynamic call center techniques will allow many savings and happy customers. One of these techniques, **metrics**, is the subject of this study guide.

Metrics

"What is a metric?" is a question that I am asked all the time. **Metric** is the term used to identify the things that we are trying to learn. Another way of describing a metric is to call it an *information study area*.

You might ask, "Why do we need metrics?" In my experience I have found **Four Traits of Effective Operations.** Trait one is the ability to respond to rapid change. Trait two is a factored organizational structure supported by defined processes. Trait three is a competent workforce that brilliantly executes the plan. Trait four is optimum decision-making based on proper information.

This fourth trait is where metrics play an essential role by providing enough information to make optimal decisions. Metrics support the call center manager. Now, what exactly do call center managers do? The following table shows the many functions that are a call center manager's responsibility.

Introduction

Call Center Manager Responsibilities	
Issues	**What they need to know and do about each issue**
People	Defined Job Responsibilities Job Compliance
Facility	Proper maintenance of the facility Facility Capable
Operations	Dependency & Relationship Key Metrics Correct & consistent running of the facility
Finance	Assets & depreciation Unit Cost Budget monitoring and tracking
Policies and regulations	Governmental Company Compliance
Planning	Utilization Scheduling Forecasting

All areas are important but some cannot be delegated and must be the prime focus of the call center manager.

The one component that is always present in effective operations is the call center manager's focus on key areas. These key areas are a subset of manager's functions. Over the years I have found that there are four areas that separate the brilliant call center managers from all the others.

First, they are better at understanding their operation.

Second, they are better at defining and identifying everyone's roles and responsibilities.

Third, they are better at assessing the center for correctness, consistency, and capability on a daily basis.

Fourth, as the previous three traits are mastered, they communicate their expectations to the management team so that the team can execute their roles and responsibilities to support the call center manager's goals.

How do you master these skills? With the Walkabout® metric blueprint as the roadmap, the effective call center managers will rapidly understand their facility inside and out, its operational dependencies, and what the key metrics are.

When effective call center managers understand the operation, they define everyone's responsibilities, communicate them to each team member, and have a medium for checking compliance. Understanding the center in this way is exactly the role of metrics.

The metric blue print is required to know all things that should be measured and monitored and then to establish the key metrics. Effective managers use the Walkabout® Method to assess the center with daily reporting. These daily reports are from measured metrics, not the opinion or voice of the staff. Initially every area of the call center is assessed. As compliance is achieved the focus shifts to the exception reporting method.

Call Center Types

The call center is the storefront for the enterprise. Call centers are classified into five types. These call center types are routing, notification, call management, processing, and content dissemination. The table below describes each one.

Call Center Types	Descriptions
Routing	Caller transfer to the correct party.
Notification	Receiver is notified of call.
Call Management	Manages the call from receipt to resolution. This type tracks and documents every step that is done to the request.
Processing	Service acts on the request. The businesses using this service include sales, order taking, billing, computer setup, etc.
Content dissemination	Gives advice and shares information over the telephone.

Introduction

The Call Center Goal

The call center manager's goal is to continually improve while at the same time making his customers happy. This goal is a never-ending journey for improvement. What is acceptable or terrific today will be considered terrible tomorrow.

Many call center managers are one-dimensional and that leads to a trouble zone. For example, by focusing on wait time and totally ignoring cost, we risk escalating our cost to an unreasonable level as we try to fix wait-time problems by simply throwing money at them. To help us avoid this kind of trouble zone, we will develop a balanced goal to use throughout this book as a means of describing our objective for call center improvement. This balanced goal must give equal weight and importance to wait time, cost, and performance.

In this book, I use the following questions to guide us in our definition of the goal. Who is our customer and what is the customer's intended purpose? A couple of words come to mind to answer these questions. One is quality and the other is value. Think about how you would define quality or value. This will give us a tool to compare your individual impression with my own definition of quality.

Quality is an attitude that flows throughout an organization. A positive approach to quality must be used to obtain the desired results. We will use a definition of quality that is much broader in scope than the classic quality definition that states that we simply exceed our customer's expectations. I will show how our broadened definition will keep us out of trouble.

Quality means more than simply meeting the customer's stated requirements. It means meeting or exceeding the customer's implied or perceived expectations as well. We must deliver the product or service to the customer when he wants it. Having a product at a competitive price but which we cannot deliver is disastrous to our quality. Not having any product is just as bad as having a defective product. This dimension of quality is being able to supply our product or service when the customer wants it.

We must also reduce our cost. For our services to remain competitive, we must ensure that the cost of our product is continually dropping. This gives us many options for directing our monetary savings. We could increase profits, reduce price, increase market share, or invest in the future, to name a few. The second dimension of quality is the continuous reduction of our cost. As we add a second dimension the word quality begins to sound like value.

Still more must be delivered to truly make the customer happy. Adding one more dimension, our objective of quality expands to understanding the customer's use of our product. Therefore, the next dimension of quality is exceeding the customer's perceived expectation of our product.

Quality is *meeting or exceeding the customer's perceived expectations and requirements while reducing cost and providing the product to the customer when he wants it*. Thus our goal is to provide value.

The three components we've discussed--performance, cost, and time-- define quality. This gives us a total definition of quality. Our principle concern is to always strive to provide the best value to the customer. The key word to describe the three dimensions of quality is **value**.

Walkabout®

The Walkabout Method has evolved over the last couple of decades. The Walkabout® gets its name from an Australian vice president of operations. Every morning we'd have coffee and then he would say, "Mate, I've got to go do my walkabout." He would walk through his facility and check every area. He was spectacular as a manager. This led to the third trait of effective managers, "they are better at assessing the operation for correctness, consistency, and capability on a daily basis."

To guarantee an effective call center, our knowledge base must be checked to assure that it is an accurate portrait of what is actually being done. Then we must confirm that the call center is doing what our knowledge base prescribes. Only then can we say we are complying with our knowledge base. From our knowledge base, we need to build a Walkabout®. To achieve an objective view, the knowledge base must be built with metrics.

In Australia, a walkabout is a wandering stroll to see the countryside. In our context, we are wandering in a controlled and disciplined way to assure a correct, consistent, and capable call center. The Walkabout®

provides the roadmap and metrics test the knowledge base. Knowledge checklists for all associates must be built from the metrics to effectively run the center.

When I have managed facilities and advised clients, my worst setbacks have come from having someone tell me he knew he was following the plan, but no one ever checked on him. We will use our Walkabouts® and metrics to answer many questions. Documenting the system through metrics gives us a context within which we measure our product and process. When a call center manager is doing a Walkabout®, he is assessing the center using metrics.

Walkabout® Method

To assist the effective manager and make his Walkabout® smoother, a method is required. Many techniques have been used over the years, with varying degrees of success. The Walkabout® Method uses change management as the overall strategy. In basic terms, hold everything stable and assess when a change occurs.

What is required is an objective means of assessing all change. These assessments must be immediate and real-time. Metrics are the key to this operational philosophy. Metrics are used here to detect change and then to assess the change. Changes that result in deterioration are eliminated. Changes that bring improvements are incorporated into a revised plan for the center.

This graphic shows that metrics are our eyes and ears for improvement. For improvement to occur change must occur. Any time a change occurs, even in the best of circumstances, the result might be negative. Thus we need a change detector and a companion for assessing every change's impact on the call center's capability; this paints the call center's total picture.

We have developed an improvement model using change management that strives to tell the call center story. Use of this new model allows us to dramatically accelerate our improvement in our call center.

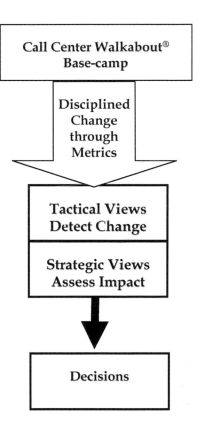

Guiding Principles

For the purposes of illustration, let's examine the field of mechanics. The study of mechanics has been marked by steady but slow increases in understanding. Here's a brief overview of the evolution of thoughts concerning motion. Understanding motion has evolved over hundreds of years. Aristotle continually improved his theories of motion. Later Galileo expanded and improved on Aristotle's theories. Later still, Newton expanded and improved on Galileo's theories, and so the scientific studies continued through history.

In the study of physics, Sir Isaac Newton stated the basic principles of motion in his book *Principia Mathematica* (1686).

- **Newton's First Principle**: Any object left alone (either at rest or at a steady state of motion) remains at a constant velocity.
- **Newton's Second Principle**: The acceleration of an object is directly proportional to the resultant force acting on the object. Any object of mass (M) encountering acceleration (A) establishes a relationship called force. Force equals mass times acceleration, or $F = MA$. A force will accelerate a small object more rapidly than it will a larger object.
- **Newton's Third Principle**: For every action on an object there is an equal and opposite reaction.

Newton's three principles are the basis for all mechanical physics, studies of motion, and mechanical engineering. How many times have you heard someone say, *"We can't change or improve this process because really, really smart people set it up"*? If Newton had believed that statement, he never would have developed the three laws of physics. Who could argue that Aristotle was not a really smart man? But Aristotle believed and taught that objects with more earth (mass) would fall faster than objects with less earth. The knowledge base had not yet progressed to the point when Newton would prove that two objects of differing mass would fall at the same rate. Newton, Aristotle, and Galileo were all smart. Newton wisely expanded and improved on both Aristotle's and Galileo's knowledge base of motion. Wise people can improve on what other wise people have done.

In his statement of the three laws of motion, Newton set up basic principles for all mechanics. These principles gave a focus to all studies that relate to mechanics. For us to begin our study of process management, we must understand the basic operations that apply to every call center facility. The Principles of Process Management give the same focus and guidance to our work that Newton's Laws brought to physics. Our Principles of Process Management are as essential to improvement as Newton's principles were to physics and motion. These principles are critical to an effective use of metrics in our call center.

First Principle of Process Management

A fundamental understanding of BOTH the product and process is essential to improvement. Both the product and the process must be described and understood individually and separately. The underlying component for improving the product is the process.

The first principle drives all improvement by stating that the underlying component for improving the product (in our case, the call center service is our "product") is the process (how we run the center). Obviously, then, we must focus our attention on the process. Increased knowledge of the product and product metrics does not equate to increased knowledge of the process. Metrics about dropped calls do not give us the knowledge of how to avoid dropped calls. Using the first principle we can build a plan of what metrics are critical and what must be monitored.

This principle will help us understand what we can and cannot manage. From a metric context the first principle shows what metrics are proactive and allows us to build a metric blueprint.

Second Principle of Process Management

Division of Labor is the framework for all aspects of decision making. It must be clearly understood to separate the policy, strategic, and tactical decisions. Operations makes the tactical decisions of running the facility. Management makes the strategic decisions of assessing the facility's suitability for the job. Executives make the policy decisions of providing the vision for the business.

The second principle is crucial to a clear understanding of call center decisions and who should make them. The policy decision makers must provide a clear business vision. This vision must include our call center and how we will treat our customers.

Based on this policy vision the strategists must provide a facility that will meet the vision. Strategic decisions are decisions in which we use our product and process knowledge to determine a goal and then obtain the means to accomplish that goal.

The tacticians must run the provided call center facility as correctly and consistently as possible. Tactical decisions are made using our product and process knowledge to assure the correct and consistent running of the operation that our strategic decision makers provided.

The metrics techniques required for these differing but complementary decision types will be different for strategists and tacticians.

Third Principle of Process Management

An effective operation must be built on a base of correctness, consistency, and capability. The strategic decision makers provide a correct facility for the tactical decision makers to run correctly. Consistency is the level at which the tactical workforce is able to hit the target. Capability is strategic in nature. It measures the facility's ability to provide what the customer wants.

These three process principles are critical to an effective use of metrics. The third principle builds the base for our change management philosophy. This base of correct, consistent, and capable form the 3Cs for our call center metrics to track.

The Goal of this Book: Knowledge Through Metrics

Our goal is to continually improve while keeping our customers happy. Our definition of quality or value is comprised of three components that must always be kept balanced. These components are:

- Performance
- Cost
- Time

Our metrics and decisions must support this goal of delighting our customer (performance) while reducing our cost (cost) and providing our product to our customers the moment they want it (time). This goal must be viewed as a never-ending journey that continues to improve all three components. No one component is more important than the others. All three must be viewed with equal importance and balance.

We will use metrics to tell the call center story for increased knowledge of our facility and operation. This knowledge through metrics must ultimately be applied for a more effective call center.

To achieve production and quality, we must meet the three quality objectives:

- Wait time
- Cost
- Performance

With these three criteria, we have a clear call center goal. We must now marshal our efforts to achieve the target goal.

Many times I hear the question, "Do you want quantity or quality?" Production or "quantity," is often mistakenly defined as keeping all agents busy, getting callers off the lines, or the number of calls handled. The only correct time to count production is when we answer the customer question perfectly, he pays us, and he is happy. The only answer to the question above, *"Do you want quality or quantity?* is that we want both quantity and quality.

Clearly, our definition of quality is extremely broad and encompassing. According to our definition, quality is comprised of three components: performance, cost, and time. Our research, analysis, and decisions must support the goal of delighting our customers (performance), while reducing our cost (cost), and providing our product to our customers the moment they want it (time). We must view this goal as a never-ending journey to continue improving all three components because no one component is more important than the others. All three must be viewed with equal importance and balance.

Having It All

Often I hear people say that you can have one or two of the three criteria of wait time, cost, and performance. To achieve all three, creativity is required.

To understand the concept of having it all, let's visit a grocery store. This is an everyday problem that we all can relate to. This also allows us to explain the concept of queuing theory in basic terms. For our example we have a grocery store with a checkout station. On this station we can process a full buggy load of groceries in eight minutes. On person mans the station and is paid $10,000 per year.

Now we have customers coming to the station for checkout. To make it easier to follow I have given each customer a number that will stay with them through the example scenario. This number matches when they arrived at the checkout station.

Customer one arrives at the checkout first and there is no wait. Customer two arrives at the checkout and has to wait the eight minutes for the first person to be completed. Then the third and fourth customers both arrive with full buggies.

Customer five arrives and only has one item. It can be processed much faster and will only take .5 minutes or 30 seconds. Customers six and seven also have one item.

In our example we process each customer in a first-in, first-out methodology. We do not attempt to apply any of the logic associated with queuing science. Wait time is a function of processing time, utilization, and processing time variability. But in our example no science has been applied, and we crudely overpower the wait time by adding more clerks.

Clerk One			
Customer	Items	Checkout Time	Wait Time
1	Full buggy	8 min	
2	Full buggy	8 min	8 min
3	Full buggy	8 min	16 min
4	Full buggy	8 min	24 min
5	One item	.5 min	32 min
6	One item	.5 min	32.5 min
7	One item	.5 min	33 min

In the table we see the queue—or line—at the checkout with the corresponding processing time and wait time respectively. We can easily see that the wait times are getting out of hand and totally unacceptable to our customers. Our average wait is 24.25 minutes with a standard deviation of 10.36 minutes when one clerk is used. This wait time is excessive and our store manager must do something to improve the situation.

Our crude solution to resolving the long wait times at the register is to add more clerks. The clerks will process the customers through the checkout line in a first-in, first-out manner. Our store manager adds one additional clerk and the resulting queues are shown in the table below.

Clerk One			
Customer	Items	Checkout Time	Wait Time
1	Full buggy	8 min	
3	Full buggy	8 min	8 min
5	One item	.5 min	16 min
7	One item	.5 min	16.5 min

Clerk Two			
Customer	Items	Checkout Time	Wait Time
2	Full buggy	8 min	
4	Full buggy	8 min	8 min
6	One item	.5 min	16 min

With two clerks processing at checkout, our average wait is 12.9 minutes. This solution has reduced the average wait time but it has increased our cost since we now have two clerks making $10,000 each. Our total cost is $20,000.

The wait time is still somewhat high, so our store manager decides to open a third line. The table below shows the impact on the wait time for each customer.

Clerk One			
Customer	Items	Checkout Time	Wait Time
1	Full buggy	8 min	
4	Full buggy	8 min	8 min
7	One item	.5 min	16 min

Clerk Two			
Customer	Items	Checkout Time	Wait Time
2	Full buggy	8 min	
5	One item	.5 min	8 min

Clerk 3			
Customer	Items	Checkout Time	Wait Time
3	Full buggy	8 min	
6	One item	.5 min	8 min

With three clerks, the average wait drops to 10.0 minutes. This approach carries a $30,000 price tag.

Express Lane Structure

Rethinking the whole grocery store checkout methodology can yield some interesting results. For this example, wait time is a function of average processing time and the processing time variability. Variability is the size difference of our checkout time. The lower the difference, the lower the wait time. Let's look again at our grocery store checkout example, but this time split our customers into two groups. One group has full buggies and members of the other group have one item each. The processing time variability for each group is zero. The processing time of the full buggy line is eight minutes. The processing time of the one item line is .5 minutes. The result of this shift in method is shown in the table below.

Full Buggy Clerk			
Customer	Items	Checkout Time	Wait Time
1	Full buggy	8 min	
2	Full buggy	8 min	8 min
3	Full buggy	8 min	16 min
4	Full buggy	8 min	24 min

Express Clerk			
Customer	Items	Checkout Time	Wait Time
5	One item	.5 min	
6	One item	.5 min	.5 min
7	One item	.5 min	1.0 min

With one full buggy clerk and an express lane clerk, the average wait drops to 9.9 minutes with a cost of $20,000.

Efficient Versus Effective

Now let's compare the two grocery store approaches. The crude but *efficient* grocery store has the three clerks fully loaded. The average wait is ten minutes and the cost is $30,000. The *effective* grocery store has a new method and structure. The effective grocery store takes a different approach of balancing both the store's needs and the customer's needs by using queuing science. One clerk is processing full buggies and the second clerk is processing one-item customers using an express lane. With this approach the average wait is 9.9 minutes and the cost is $20,000.

The table below compares our crude approach to the express lane approach where queuing science has been applied.

	Crude Approach	Express Lane Approach
Number of clerks	3 clerks	2 clerks
Cost	$30,000	$20,000
Wait time Average	10 minutes	9.9 minutes

In every aspect of the above example the express lane approach is better. Our express lane may not be *efficient* at the micro level (on occasion our express clerk might have to wait for a customer with the requisite low number of groceries), but the total store is more *effective* using the express lane approach.

Queuing Science

Queuing science allows us to have it all through an understanding of processing time average and variability. The closer the processing times are to each other, the lower the wait time. Standard deviation is a measure of variability. The closer the variability (monitored by standard deviation) is to zero, the less difference in our checkout times.

Now we will apply what we learned in the grocery store example to call centers. In the 1910s when the first call centers were built all operators did the exact same routing task, thus all calls were about the same duration. Call variation stayed a non-issue for decades. With the advent of modern centers with multiple tasks, call processing time variation became a major issue.

Today we have the five call center types--routing, notification, call management, processing, and content dissemination. Science and metrics allow us to determine what could form a call center express lane. These call center express lanes keep wait times down, reduce cost, and provide better performance in our responses to customers or users.

The grocery store checkout example showed the impact of the drivers of wait time. Wait time is a function of the utilization of the clerk, the processing time average, and the processing time variability. The Pollaczek-Kyntchin equation takes all three issues into account and calculates wait time. In a modern call center caller waits are a function of agent utilization, call processing time average, and call processing time variability.

The graph below shows us the wait time results. The horizontal axis of the graph shows utilizations from 0% to 100%. The vertical axis shows the calculated wait time from 0 minutes to 350 minutes. The line graph shown is for a call that has an average processing time of three minutes. The call processing time variation is from two minutes to four minutes. The spread is relatively small.

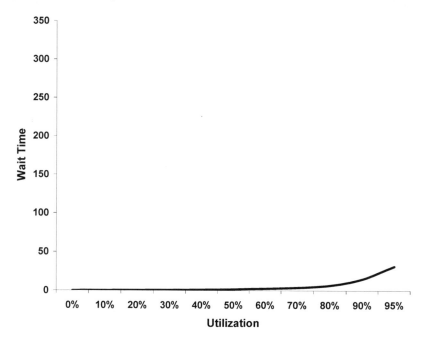

The curve stays very close to zero and only begins to rise as we approach 90+% utilizations. With most calls being close to the average, our wait times are low and manageable.

Next we will use the same graph but add one more curve. The second curve is the dashed line. It represents the change in variability from call to call. This call-to-call variation produces a larger spread around the average processing time of three minutes. The call variation for one call may go as high as 15 minutes and then drop to zero minutes. The processing time for an individual call is between zero and 15 minutes.

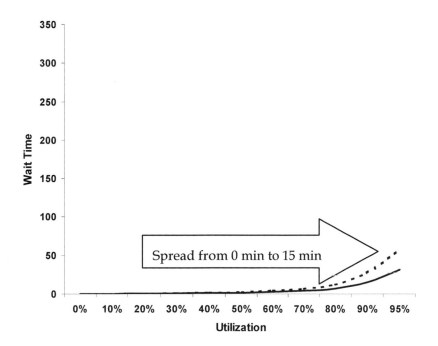

As the spread from call to call increases, the wait times begin to grow past 70% utilization. Comparing the first curve with minimal call processing time variation to the second situation with higher variation, we see that we must have lower utilizations to keep the comparable wait times of the low variation.

A third curve is added to our graph. This curve has a very wide spread between calls. The curve represents an extremely high variability ranging from 90 minutes down to zero minutes. The call processing time for an individual call will be somewhere between the zero minute and 90 minute spread.

As the spread from call to call increases, the wait times begin to grow past 30% utilization, and the curve shows wait times increasing rapidly.

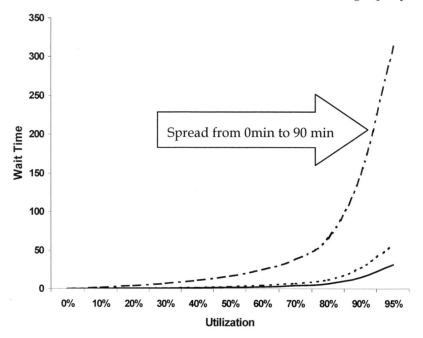

Comparing the first curve with minimal call processing time variation to the second situation with moderate variation, we see that we must have lower utilizations to keep the comparable wait times of the low variation. When we include high variation the agent utilization must be low.

Call Processing: 3 minutes			
Call Variation	Low	Moderate	High
Agent Utilization	80%	60%	20%
Caller Wait Time	4 minute	4 minute	4 minute

The table above shows a comparison of variations and their impact on wait time, agent utilization, and cost.

In the grocery store example, by understanding the wait-time drivers and building express lanes that took the processing time average, variability, and utilization into account, we were able to reduce cost, reduce wait time, and provide better service. We can truly have it all in our call center when we apply queuing science.

Effective Call Centers Must be Scientifically Engineered

Let's go back to our simple grocery store example. A very effective manager can still have a store that is not effective. If our store is set up according to the crude model, with all clerks doing every job and not minimizing the processing time variability, the store manager can only add or remove clerks. The store manager can only be as effective as the store design.

The irony in this example is that it took 70 years for grocery store chains to appreciate the subtleties and the need to monitor and manage processing time variability. It is unrealistic to expect the store manager to also design or redesign the store. Can we really expect the store manager to develop effective aisle flows, product placement, pricing, discounts, etc? An effective store design must be strategically engineered.

The store manager should expect that the store has already been well designed and engineered. Our call center managers should expect the same. The call center design must be periodically reevaluated to assure that our engineering design is still adequate for the policy vision.

My **Four Traits of Effective Operations** were the ability to respond to rapid change, a factored organizational structure (express lanes) supported by defined processes, a competent workforce that brilliantly executes the plan, and optimum decision-making based on proper information. Strategic engineering is required for the first two traits of responding to rapid change and express lanes with defined processes. The last two traits (brilliant execution and optimal decision-making) help the tactical decision-makers to manage the scientifically engineered call center. With a well-engineered store checkout or call center we can expect our operation to be managed effectively.

Engineering provides the strategic facility that matches the policy vision. Operations must provide a competent workforce to brilliantly execute the plan. To run an effective operation the managers must trust the strategic engineers to have done their job well. Any decision-making must be based on proper information, better known as metrics.

Call Center Metrics

Change Management

For improvement to occur, a base-camp of product and process knowledge is essential. In the introduction, we discussed the need for strategic and tactical correctness, consistency, and capability. These are the three Cs that form the foundation of your call center. We call this the Walkabout® base-camp, and it provides the essential elements for an effective organization. In a correct, consistent, and capable call center operation metrics provide the means for improvement.

First, metrics must tell the story of the call center. We will need special tools for the tactical job of noting change. We will also need strategic tools for assessing the impact of every change. Our method for improvement is called change management.

Call Center Decisions

The second principle states that *the Division of Labor is the framework for all aspects of decision-making. It must be clearly understood to separate the policy, strategic, and tactical decisions. Operations makes the tactical decisions of running the facility. Management makes the strategic decisions of assessing the facility's suitability for the job. Executives make the policy decisions of providing the vision for the business.* We must understand Division of Labor to know what information to provide in the call center.

Division of Labor includes the three types of decisions: policy, strategy, and tactics. Each are fundamentally different and require different report formats, but all three must be linked into a cohesive package.

Policy defines the business vision and how the business will treat customers and users. This serves as the starting point and all decisions must support the policy vision. The call center will make strategic and tactical decisions only, but they still must support the policies.

The two types of call center decisions, strategic and tactical, require fundamentally different types of information. Operations, making tactical decisions, requires one type of metric reporting while the call center manager, making strategic decisions, requires a different type of metric report. The two metric reports (tactical and strategic) also work together as a team. The following table is a recap of Division of Labor.

	Division of Labor	
	Operations	Management
Accountability	The correct and consistent running of the call center facility	Finding customers who will buy our products
Responsibility	Running the scientifically engineered provided call center facility correctly and consistently	Providing the call center facility that will produce what the customer wants and meets the policy vision of the business
Functions	Detect changes	Assess the Impact of changes
Missions	Control	Capability
Decisions	Tactical	Strategic
Who	Agents, Supervisors	Call Center Managers and Directors

Call center managers make several kinds of strategic decisions including which resource to use, when to use the resource, and where to use the resource. Strategy, for our context, is planning and providing the correct resources at the correct time and at the correct place. Strategic personnel should be held accountable for developing a plan to meet our needs. They must determine what kind of facility will meet the company's needs and then build it. The strategic personnel should be held accountable for how well the facility they provide meets the company's needs.

Agents and call center supervisors make the tactical decisions for running the provided facility as correctly and consistently as possible. The proper term for their efforts is control. When we say that we are "in control," we are only talking about operational issues. The term in control means that the facility is running consistently. When we understand the concept of control, we realize that the objective of operations is the correct and consistent running of the currently available and existing facility. Operations must keep a focus on the tactical needs by making tactical decisions and conducting tactical analysis.

Clearly then, we must have tools available to us to measure the call center facility's unique metrics both strategically and tactically.

Call Center Metric Report Format

A standard format makes reading the story of our call center simple and easy. One format is used for tacticians and a second format is for the strategist.

The tactical reports that detect change are time-oriented charts as shown below. The tactical personnel detect changes using this chart.

Tactical Reporting

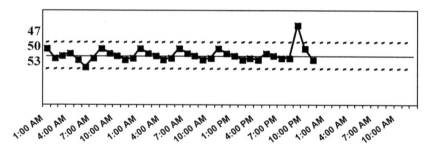

The strategic reports that assess each change are called capability studies. This report uses the data from the tactical charts to assess the facility's capability when run correctly and consistently by the tactician.

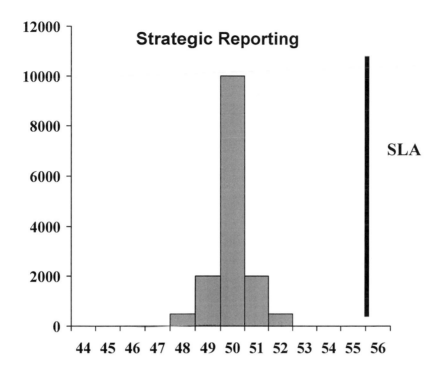

Having a standard format for metrics makes their use much easier. A supervisor or manager can move, migrate, transfer, or be promoted, and still know the reporting method.

Tactical Reports for Running the Call Center

In a call center, calls are constantly coming in. The reporting format called control charts was designed to track these situations. Control charts are used to monitor the operation and to detect when a change occurs. Control charts provide the mechanism to determine whether a particular metric is consistent. They could also be called "consistency charts," "change detectors," or "cause detectors." A control chart functions as an alarm system to alert us to changes and deviations. Changes can take the form of either improvements or deterioration of the process. Control charts cannot identify whether change is improvement or deterioration. A control chart's mission is very specialized-- to identify change.

When a control chart detects a change, two things must happen before action can be taken. First, the tactician must do research as to the cause of the change. Second, the strategic decision-maker must assess the impact of the change on the center, callers, and our service. With this information in hand, a decision as to a course of action can be made.

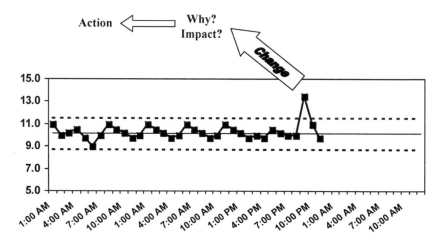

Control charts are operations tools for the supervisor or agent, they are not reports for management. Service Level Agreements, SLAs, are wonderful tools for strategic decisions. Since SLAs are strategic in nature, they *never* appear on a control chart. Control charts are for the tactical decisions of tracking the consistency of the call center metrics and for detecting change. Control charts must be used in conjunction with the strategic reports called capability studies.

Strategic Reports for Assessing the Call Center

Capability studies assess how well our call center matches what the customer wants. These studies assume the call center metrics are in control.

When we understand the concept of capability, we realize that the objective of management is to assure that we are providing a facility that can make the product or provide the service that the customer wants. Management must find the means or facility to supply operations. Strategic decisions are categorized as defining and obtaining the appropriate resources, and then determining when and where to use them.

Management uses strategies and strategic decisions to continually evaluate the adequacy of the facility for making what the customer wants. This strategic decision is based on the information provided from the capability study. If the facility is not capable, a strategic decision must be made concerning a proper course of action.

This is an example of a capability chart. Use a graph like this for management reports.

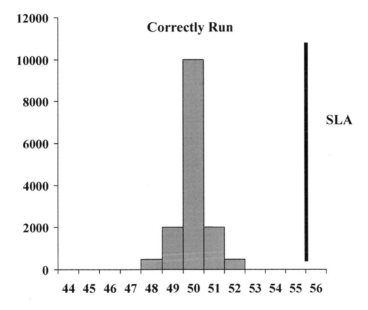

Determining the facility is clearly a strategic function. Strategic decisions involve defining and obtaining appropriate resources and then determining when and where to use those resources. The capability study gives management the information it needs to make appropriate decisions.

Chapter Two

Strategist and Tactician Working as a Team

Strategic and tactical roles are very different but they must work in harmony and trust. Understanding who is responsible for each task is key to a successful organization. If a supervisor tries taking on every role, he risks not being successful in any role. Violating the second principle by compounding the responsibilities of management with those of operations, leads to chaotic decision-making.

When both strategic and tactical personnel understand and do their jobs, they form a team. The proper support metrics must come together to build a finely honed partnership that allows for good, effective, clear decisions.

Many companies are frustrated because they never see results or improvement. They don't see gains and they wonder why the metrics have failed to yield results. Actually, the answer lies in they way they have used metrics—in particular, the way they have used SPC. The best format and reporting techniques monitoring the wrong things will not yield the desired improvements. Proper technique monitoring the right study areas is required for metrics to work.

Metrics Must Tell a Story

When you read a short story, article, or book, you are told a story by the author. Effective stories paint a vivid picture of what the author is visualizing. Authors have a style that they use in their writing, and an outline that ties all the points, issues, and story line together. Like any good author, we must develop a style and have a call center outline. Then our call center metrics will tell the story for our decision-makers.

The style that we will use is called Statistical Process Control or SPC. This style of "writing" is composed of two reporting methods--control charts and capability studies. This style will give us a common format for preparing all of our metric reports. The call center outline will be in the form of a schematic called the Walkabout® Metric Blueprint.

With the style and outline working together we can tell the story of our call center.

Common Format

The common style or format is composed of a strategic component and a tactical component. These two components must work together in a timely and disciplined fashion.

Tactical reports are called control charts. They support the tactical decisions of correctly and consistently running the facility. The chart alerts the tactical decision-makers as to a change in the profile of the call center metrics. Remember, change can be either an improvement or deterioration. A control chart's horizontal axis is a time sequence presentation, while the vertical axis is the metric unit of measure.

This is an example of a control chart.

Tactical Reporting

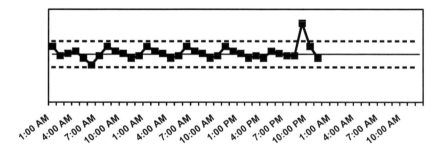

When a change is detected, as shown above, the tactician should determine the cause and alert the strategic decision-maker that a change has occurred.

This is an example of a capability chart.

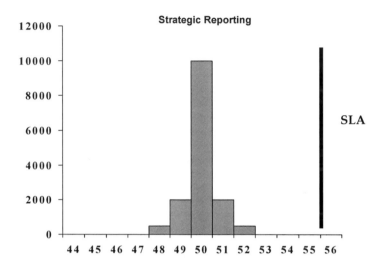

The strategic reporting is called a capability study and it is presented in the form of a histogram. The horizontal axis is the metric unit of measure while the vertical axis shows the number of occurrences. The strategist must use this tool to assess the impact of the change on the call center.

By having a standard format, personnel migration from area to area requires no retraining in how to read a report. With both metric formats working together we can fully understand the metric. Now we need to understand it in context with all the other metrics in our center. This total understanding is where our call center outline, called a Walkabout® Metric Blueprint, comes into play.

Good Metrics Misused

A "reactionary" approach means that we begin our causal research only after a change in the product has been identified or customer complaints have been noted. Said another way, we are reacting to the problems after they occur. Focusing on results allows defects to be made, thus driving cost and delays up. This is a misguided approach that I refer to as "Statistical Biscuit Control" or SBC.

In my book, *Optimize Your Operation*, I told the story of my mother learning the art of biscuit making from my grandmother. Grandma was an accomplished biscuit chef. She knew to adjust the oven as the biscuits were baking to ensure a perfect product every time. However, if my grandmother had used the SBC approach, she would have waited for the biscuit control chart to alert her that the biscuits were burnt. There would be many burnt biscuits and unhappy family members as my grandmother reacted to the control chart for each batch.

The reactionary approach waits until the product has shifted before any action is taken. In our story, the number of burnt biscuits determined all decisions. In a call center setting burnt biscuits are analogous to tracking and responding to customer complaints. Developing a metric blueprint is the first step away from poor, reactionary decisions.

Outline

A few authors have the natural ability to just start writing words, sentences, and paragraphs, with the story flowing off their pens. The rest of us require a plan as shown through an outline. This outline paints the picture that we want told in our story. Similarly, the call center metrics need to tell the call center's story. The Walkabout® Metric Blueprint is our outline. The metric blueprint provides a guide for process sequence, upstream and downstream causal dependencies, key metrics, and target settings.

The first Principle of Process Management explains the interconnection between the product and process. *A fundamental understanding of BOTH the product and process is essential to improvement. Both the product and the process must be described and understood individually and separately. The underlying component for improving the product is the process.*

The Walkabout® is a schematic of the call center depicted through a dependency diagram.

Grandma's Baking Outline

The chart below is the Walkabout® Dependency Diagram for baking Grandma's biscuits. The dependency diagram shows the sequence of activities.

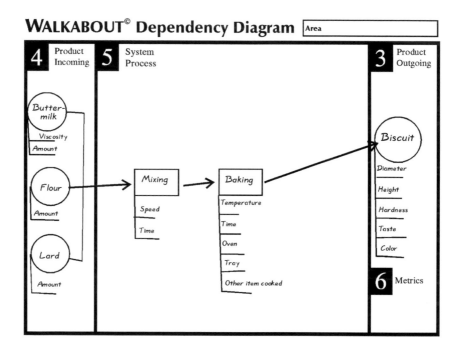

The dependency diagram is shown with circles for the products (think of biscuits) and rectangles for the processes (imagine an oven for baking). The schematic shows the sequence in which each activity occurs. This picture makes the learning process easy. Hanging from the products and processes are legs that have the metrics that we will want to study. The dependency diagram and the metric legs form the blueprint.

The Walkabout® describes the dependencies and defines the metrics. With the Walkabout® in place, we have a tool that will give us both a short and a long-range plan for metrics. Now let's develop call center Walkabouts® and see how they are used for each of call center type.

Telling the Call Center Story

The call center story is first told at a high level using an umbrella Walkabout®. The following diagram is the umbrella Walkabout® for a routing call center, showing its one major activity called triage.

Metrics must include those that are done manually by a person as well as those that have been automated. The automated triage will include call director, ACD, and IVR. Automated functions need metrics for a clear understanding of how they are performing. Metrics are just as crucial for automated tasks and processes as for those that people are doing.

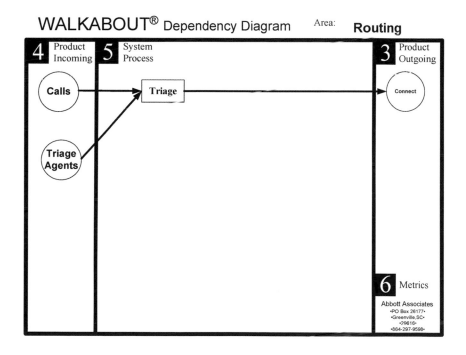

The umbrella Walkabout® must expand to accommodate each major function. This routing center only has the one function of triage. For each triage activity we draw a box to identify the process step. The first process is "answer the call" so we draw our first box. The second step is to assess the question, the third step is to assess the severity, and the final step is to route the call to the appropriate area. Each of these areas is drawn on the diagram. This schematic shows the sequence of events. A possible companion to this dependency diagram would be a clearly defined script if it is a person doing the routing.

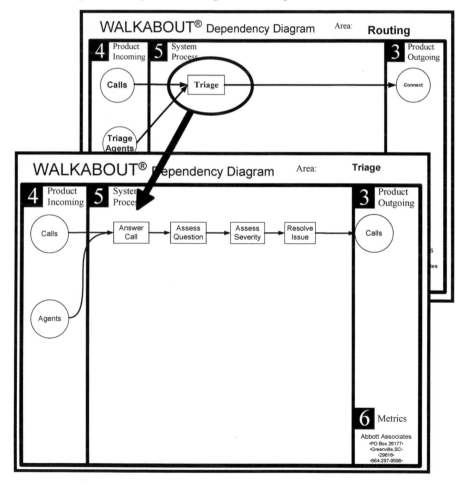

This dependency diagram defines the correct method.

Next we add the metrics that we would view as important for running the call center function. Whether we can actually obtain the metric measurement is not the issue. This identifies what metrics are needed to run our call center effectively.

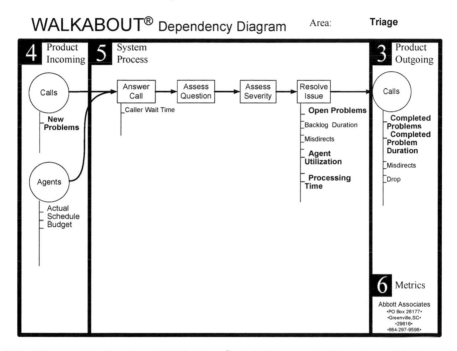

This diagram is the triage Walkabout® with the metric blueprint added.

We have covered the umbrella Walkabout® and Walkabout® for the routing call center. The notification and call management center types are similar to the routing center with a few minor differences. Let's explore the differences so that we can use the same Walkabout® for all three call center types.

The routing call center makes immediate or "hot" call transfers to the appropriate person. The difference between the routing and notification center is how the transfer is made. The routing center is a hot transfer while the notification has a time delay for the transfer. The notification center is the same as the routing center with a method for holding notes during the call time delay.

The call management center type adds a tracking aspect to the routing center. The call management center not only transfers the call but also follows the progress of the call status to make sure that the call is handled in a proper manner. Think of a 911 operator staying on the line even though the police have been dispatched. The call management center adds an additional requirement of a tracking system for noting all the activities and transactions associated with the call.

With these differences noted, the three call center types can be grouped together into a triage function shown in the umbrella Walkabout®. The detail Walkabout® and metric blue print defined for the routing center type can also be used for the notification and the call management center types.

The triage metrics to include are the number of calls opened, the number of calls closed, the length of time actually processing the call, how long the call took to resolve or its duration, agent utilization, the number of calls still open, and the time the open calls have been open. These key metrics should be viewed as the minimum to get started and clearly this must be customized to your center.

The following two diagrams are the umbrella Walkabouts® for processing and content dissemination centers. Processing centers typically deal with information coming in. Content dissemination centers typically distribute information in an outbound direction. The processes are very similar as the following Walkabouts® show. Since the two centers operate so similarly, we'll just construct the Walkabout® for the Content Dissemination Center.

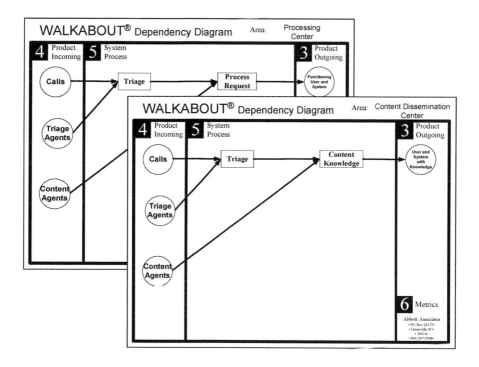

The Walkabout® below shows the processes steps and the metric blueprint for the triage phase of the content dissemination center.

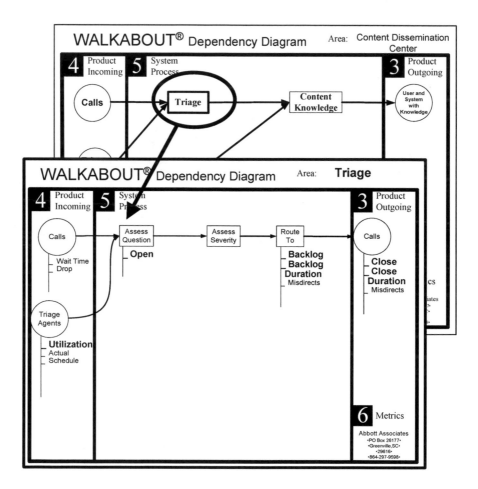

The key metrics discussed earlier, customized to your center, should be viewed as the minimum to get started.

The Walkabout® below shows the processes steps and the metric blueprint for the content phase of the content dissemination center.

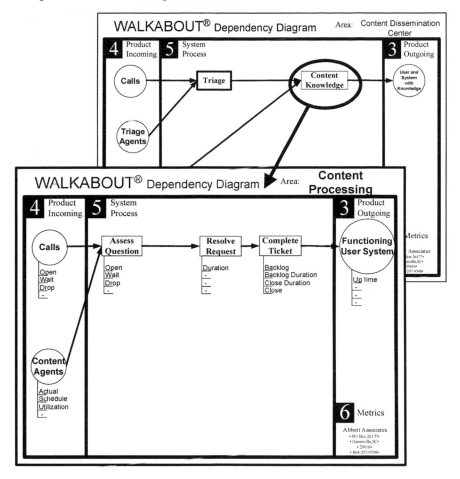

Once again, the same key metrics are the starting set of metrics in most call centers.

Metric Balance

The Walkabout® keeps the metrics in balance. Once we have added the metrics to the Walkabout® Dependency Diagram, we have an excellent tool to see where the metrics are. We can see if we have many outgoing product metrics but only a few incoming product and process metrics. Metric balance allows us to understand the total system.

Should our diagram have significantly more metric legs on any one area than another, the metrics are out of balance. Too much of our focus is being placed on one area. Incorrectly balanced metrics will lead to inappropriate action. If the biscuits are burnt, we will want to take some corrective action. If no oven metrics are available, we will not know where to work or what corrective action to take. Generally this lack of information seldom stops us from taking some kind of action even if the action is unwarranted or wrong. Without some understanding of the oven (process), any action we take to correct the burnt biscuits will be wrong.

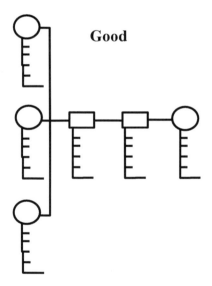

Good

A correct balance of information would result in a metric blueprint as shown to the left. It is balanced or has close to the same number of metrics for all areas. This will provide a tremendous amount of information. We can learn in a balanced way about both the product and the process.

Chapter Three:
Monitoring Metrics

Metrics are the informational eyes of the decision-maker. Since we must make decisions in the face of uncertainty, metrics offer the tools to assist in these situations. Our objective must always be to provide as clear a picture of the data as possible while also keeping our volume of numbers as low as possible. To assure that we never present improper information, we must identify the proper procedures and the areas that will cause flawed information.

Reporting and Analysis Flaws

The objective of analysis is an increased knowledge base. Data analysis provides the cohesion to build the strategies and tactics that will drive our improvement. Analysis must always be conducted using defined procedures so that we will avoid any tainted results.

It is not enough to simply trace the history of events. Analysis also must uncover the causes of the effects. Since an effect is not caused by simply one item, our analysis must continuously strive to uncover more of the causes and how much of the effect can be assigned to any one cause.

The analysis must endeavor to uncover the who, what, where, and when of the cause that is driving the effect. This is not a one-time effort but a continuing and on-going search to increase our knowledge base. We must clearly understand and adhere to the science of how to analyze the who, what, where, and when so that we avoid any inaccurate information that might drive us to make improper decisions.

Our objective is to assure that we understand the potential flaws of improperly prepared data. In order to avoid these costly mistakes, we must have a clear set of guidelines so that we can prepare information that allows us to make accurate and intelligent decisions. Improper technique and improper grouping are the two main statistical reporting flaws.

We must understand and use proper techniques while we avoid the mistakes caused by using improper techniques. Technique is the systematic procedure by which a complex or scientific task is accomplished. Statistics brings to us a consistent and common language when we correctly prepare our numbers with proper technique.

Grouping can lead to a different set of problems. These problems must be clearly understood so that all of our studies will use proper groups. Grouping is a number of individual things considered together because of similarities.

Reports are often used to show when things are bad. Being a child of the 50s, I grew up watching TV. One of my favorite programs was "Dragnet." The main character was Joe Friday played by Jack Webb. His watchword and the theme of the program was always "Just the Facts Ma'am." We need to pattern ourselves after Joe Friday, neither looking for good nor bad, but always looking for the facts.

This chapter will explain proper statistical technique for monitoring metrics, while a later chapter will clarify the need for and types of grouping required for proper information to be presented. This same grouping required for proper reports will also be used to determine express lane candidates.

Analysis Practice

Our first study will revolve around a common problem. We will analyze the call volume for a call center over time. The table below shows the call volume for the years 1980, 1981, 1982, and part of the year 1983.

For statistics to work effectively, a clear objective must be stated. Therefore, the information gained from this study will be used to plan the required facilities for the call center.

Call Volume				
	1980	1981	1982	1983
JANUARY	2749	4081	4982	3936
FEBRUARY	5405	5004	4299	5024
MARCH	3936	2708	3793	3239
APRIL	2232	2423	1870	
MAY	1079	1493	1514	
JUNE	1330	2197	1713	
JULY	2616	2918	1890	
AUGUST	2820	2041	1897	
SEPTEMBER	2321	2041	1923	
OCTOBER	1583	1494	1316	
NOVEMBER	1877	1859	1843	
DECEMBER	3439	3936	2919	

Proper statistical technique requires that we monitor three components—central tendency, variability, and distribution. Each component
must be understood and used correctly. Our first tool will monitor the
data's central tendency or balance point.

What Is Balance?

When we were children, we used to play on a seesaw or teeter-totter.
One of the main things we tried to do was get the seesaw to balance two
people on opposite ends of a board. The spot the board rests on is called
the fulcrum.

45

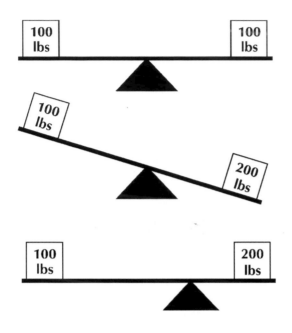

When both sides weigh equal amounts, the fulcrum is positioned in the center.

When one side weighs more than the other, the board will tilt toward the side of the heavier weight.

By moving the fulcrum toward the heavier weight, we can find a position where the seesaw will once again balance.

This balance point is critical information in many fields like physics and mechanical engineering. Balance associated with numeric measurements is essential to statistics. The balance point is called **central tendency**.

Monitors of Central Tendency

Since central tendency is critical to understanding numeric measurements, monitors of it must be established. The first monitor of central tendency is **average**. Average is *a point estimate of the measurement of the central tendency of the data*. Average is a statistical tool to monitor the central tendency and is also referred to as the mean or the arithmetic mean. All the different names—average, mean, and arithmetic mean-- are describing the same monitor. Average is the balance point of all the data points giving equal weight to each value.

Average

The average monitors central tendency. Average divides the sum of the measurements by the number of measurements. The algebraic expression for average is

$$\frac{X_1 + X_2 + X_3 + ...X_N}{N}$$ where N is the last data point.

To compute the average call volume for the year 1980, individual call volume for each of the 12 months is added and then divided by the total number of months (12). The 1980 total calls are 31,387 which is then divided by 12 to arrive at the average of 2,616 calls per month. The following chart shows how the average is representing the central tendency of call volume data for 1980.

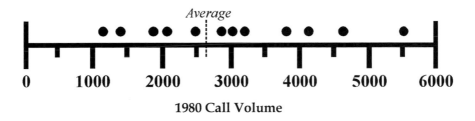

1980 Call Volume

Note how clearly the average shows the center point of call volume.

Never use average as a stand-alone measure of a set of values. Central tendency should not be discussed without a companion monitor of variability.

Averages can be misleading. The three sets of data below are intended to demonstrate that simply looking at an average can give an erroneous impression.

Motel Chain Pricing			
Motel Locations	**A**	**B**	**C**
Greenville, SC	25	25	10
Charlotte, NC	27	25	15
Atlanta, GA	24	25	20
Birmingham, AL	25	25	25
Nashville, TN	26	25	20
Indianapolis, IN	26	25	15
Louisville, KY	24	25	10
Lexington, KY	23	2	25
Cincinnati, OH	24	25	35
Columbus, OH	26	25	15
Denver, CO	27	25	40
Las Vegas, NV	23	25	35
Dallas, TX	25	25	30
Los Angeles, Ca	25	25	25
San Francisco, CA	24	56	30
Newark, NJ	26	25	35
Toledo, OH	25	25	40
Average	$25	$25	$25

Suppose we are trying to compare the price point of three motel chains. Notice that all three of the motel chains wind up with exactly the same average of $25 per night, but all the values of the data set are radically different. The first set of values is relatively close to the average. The second set has two values extremely removed from the other values. The third set has a widely dispersed set of values. The only common link between values is that they all have an average of $25.

My family has convinced me that vacations can be a wonderful experience. We have planned and been on several vacations over recent years. Imagine planning a vacation's sleeping-room cost based on the previous improperly prepared motel statistics. The stand-alone averages create a false picture that could cause the cost to be way above our expected cost. An otherwise wonderful vacation is destroyed when our vacation money is exhausted. Statistics must provide a clear summary picture of our numbers. Improperly prepared statistical technique must be avoided to assure that these kinds of prediction mistakes are avoided. We must always get a complete picture of our data. Nothing is wrong with the average--it simply shows only part of the picture.

Now let's expand our knowledge and add another statistical component that is needed to complement the average. This component is the amount or magnitude of spread associated with our measurements.

Magnitude of Spread

We have seen from the motel example that an average by itself can be very misleading. This would be like saying that all people who weigh the same amount look the same. As our illustration shows, the two individuals pictured are very different. One person has a spread up top, and the other has a lower spread. If we were analyzing people's weights, we would want to make sure that we had an additional technique to monitor this spread. The magnitude of this spread can be crucial to our view of a person.

When we are doing statistical analysis, a technique for monitoring spread is required as well. The name for the magnitude of the spread is **variability**. Next we will begin to discuss a series of techniques for monitoring variability or the magnitude of the spread.

Variability

We need to have a way of distinguishing the difference between the three sets of motels from the prior discussion. The means of doing this is called monitoring the variability. Our first technique for monitoring the variability of the measurements is by viewing the highest and lowest values of the data.

When using minimum and maximum data, two values are always required. This can be reduced by using the distance between the maximum and minimum values. This distance is called the **range** value. Sometimes the range is abbreviated to R value.

Range is a measure of the variability of a set of numbers. The smaller the range, the lower the variability, or the amount of spread.

Using the call volume data to compute the range for the year 1980, the highest value for the call volume is 5,405 and the lowest value is 1,079. The range for 1980 call volume equals $X_{Max} - X_{Min}$. The values can then be placed in the equation to compute the range. The 1980 range is 4,326 calls. The chart below shows our monthly call volume on a graph along with the average, maximum, minimum, and range values.

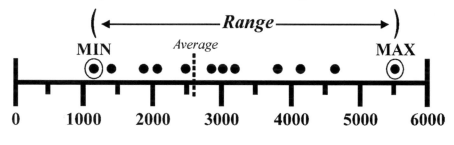

1980 Call Volume

The Interpretation and Use of Range

As the range increases, the magnitude of the variability (spread) increases. Should the range be zero, all values are the same and the average is a perfect indicator of each data point. The larger the range, the more variable the data. As the range increases, the average becomes a less precise indicator of the actual values.

The three sets of data in the motel chart demand some monitor of variability to clearly depict the different chains.

Motel Chain Pricing			
Motel Locations	**A**	**B**	**C**
Greenville, SC	25	25	10
Charlotte, NC	27	25	15
Atlanta, GA	24	25	20
Birmingham, AL	25	25	25
Nashville, TN	26	25	20
Indianapolis, IN	26	25	15
Louisville, KY	24	25	10
Lexington, KY	23	2	25
Cincinnati, OH	24	25	35
Columbus, OH	26	25	15
Denver, CO	27	25	40
Las Vegas, NV	23	25	35
Dallas, TX	25	25	30
Los Angeles, Ca	25	25	25
San Francisco, CA	24	56	30
Newark, NJ	26	25	35
Toledo, OH	25	25	40
Average	$25	$25	$25
Maximum	27	56	40
Minimum	32	2	10
Range	4	54	30

By using range and average together, we can begin to understand the differences in the three sets of data. Chain A has a mean cost of $25 and a range of $4. This drives us to the conclusion that Chain A's rates are all close to the mean. Chain B has a mean cost of $25 and a range of $54. We would conclude that Chain B's rates are very widely spread. Chain C has a mean cost of $25 and a range of $30. We would conclude that Chain C's rates are also widely spread.

Since the range values for both Chain B and Chain C are high, we might conclude that both chains charge similar rates. We can see by analyzing the data, however, that the costs of B and C are very different. Chain B has two very extreme values with the remaining rates all being equal to

$25. All of Chain C's rates are different. Therefore, the range value fails us in differentiating between these two motel chains.

We must always get a complete picture of our data. Nothing is wrong with the average, but it only tells part of the story. To add more precision to our study, we must monitor both central tendency and variability together. Neither one can be used without the other.

Properly prepared statistical information can be a wonderful tool for estimates and predictions for all decision-making, including our vacation plans. Now our family can anticipate a pleasant vacation because the statistics have painted a more vivid picture that now includes both central tendency and variability. Our plans now can be made with reliable and predictable results while avoiding the disaster of exceeding our planned vacation budget.

	Call Volume			
	1980	1981	1982	1983
JANUARY	2749	4081	4982	3936
FEBRUARY	5405	5004	4299	5024
MARCH	3936	2708	3793	3239
APRIL	2232	2423	1870	
MAY	1079	1493	1514	
JUNE	1330	2197	1713	
JULY	2616	2918	1890	
AUGUST	2820	2041	1897	
SEPTEMBER	2321	2041	1923	
OCTOBER	1583	1494	1316	
NOVEMBER	1877	1859	1843	
DECEMBER	3439	3936	2919	
Average	2616	2683	2497	4066
Range	4326	3511	3666	1785

The call volume average and range work together to allow us to begin planning our call center needs. The average for 1980 is 2,616 calls with a range of 4,326 calls. A range of this magnitude in relation to its average is quite large. Our conclusion would indicate that large swings from month to month should be anticipated if 1980 is representative of the future.

The year 1981 also has a large range of 3,511 calls in relation to its average of 2,683 calls; this reinforces our conclusion from the analysis of 1980. Similarly, 1982 has a large range of 3,666 calls in relation to the average of 2,497.

Since 1983's call volume is incomplete, no conclusion should be made from the data. To increase our information about the spread of the data, a more advanced method of monitoring variability is required. This improved method should include all of the data.

Standard Deviation as a Monitor of Variability

In many respects, standard deviation is simply a more elaborate range calculation. Thus the method for interpreting standard deviation is similar to the method for interpreting range. When X-bar is used as the symbol for average, the equation for calculating standard deviation reads as follows. Since the formula is included in most computer software, the mechanics are really not a concern.

The following table shows our hotel chain comparison, adding the standard deviation for each.

Motel Chain Pricing			
Motel Locations	**A**	**B**	**C**
Greenville, SC	25	25	10
Charlotte, NC	27	25	15
Atlanta, GA	24	25	20
Birmingham, AL	25	25	25
Nashville, TN	26	25	20
Indianapolis, IN	26	25	15
Louisville, KY	24	25	10
Lexington, KY	23	2	25
Cincinnati, OH	24	25	35
Columbus, OH	26	25	15
Denver, CO	27	25	40
Las Vegas, NV	23	25	35
Dallas, TX	25	25	30
Los Angeles, Ca	25	25	25
San Francisco, CA	24	56	30
Newark, NJ	26	25	35
Toledo, OH	25	25	40
Average	$25	$25	$25
Maximum	$27	$56	$40
Minimum	$32	$2	$10
Range	$4	$54	$30
Standard Deviation	$1	$9	$10

Now our additional monitor of variability—standard deviation--should be used. Remember, this value must be used in conjunction with average.

For the three motel chains in the table, we would draw the following conclusions. Chain A's average cost of $25 and standard deviation of $1 indicates that the rates in this chain are very tightly clustered. Chain B's average cost of $25 but standard deviation of $9 indicates that the rates in this chain are widely spread. Chain C's average cost of $25 and standard deviation of $10 indicates that the rates in this chain are also very widely spread.

For this example, when we use monitors of central tendency and variability, Motel A is clearly different from Motels B and C. By viewing the actual rates for Motels B and C, we see that additional techniques may be required for analysis of these motels. We will discuss these techniques later in this chapter.

Using what we've learned about variability, let's revisit our call center problem.

	Call Volume			
	1980	1981	1982	1983
JANUARY	2749	4081	4982	3936
FEBRUARY	5405	5004	4299	5024
MARCH	3936	2708	3793	3239
APRIL	2232	2423	1870	
MAY	1079	1493	1514	
JUNE	1330	2197	1713	
JULY	2616	2918	1890	
AUGUST	2820	2041	1897	
SEPTEMBER	2321	2041	1923	
OCTOBER	1583	1494	1316	
NOVEMBER	1877	1859	1843	
DECEMBER	3439	3936	2919	
Average	**2616**	**2683**	**2497**	**4066**
Range	**4326**	**3511**	**3666**	**1785**
Std Dev	**1211**	**1112**	**1211**	**900**

The call volume average, range, and standard deviation work together to allow us to plan our future center needs even better. The standard deviation for the three years of 1980, 1981, and 1982 are very similar: 1,211; 1,112; and 1,211 respectively. This will allow us to conclude that our monitor of variability is a good measure. The magnitude of the standard deviation is still very high in relation to the averages, thus forcing us to plan for large swings in call volume each month.

In the statistical community the term sigma, shown as σ, is used to signify the population's variability. The term mu, shown as μ, is used to signify the population's central tendency. The standard deviation is abbreviated as S or Std while variance uses S^2.

Metric Measurement

Measuring our metric is key to learning. Lord Kelvin once said, "When you can measure what you are speaking about, and express it in numbers, you know something about it. But when you cannot express it in numbers, your knowledge is of a meager and unsatisfactory kind."

There will be several methods for capturing and measuring our call center metrics. Don't expect that every metric must be captured automatically. Sometimes simple counts can provide valuable information.

Use the data in your phone system, but take care to remember that in most call centers much work is done before and after the phone conversation. This time must be included. Also, if you have a ticketing system it can be a gold mine of information about your center.

Be sure you take measurements for individual calls. Many metrics date back to the days of the telephone operator when all calls required the same action and the call durations were about the same. Then an average of an interval (like an hour) was useful. In today's multifunction call centers the call durations have significant variation. The only way to track and monitor that variation is having the individual call readings (i.e. call duration, wait time, etc.) Understanding and managing this variation allows us to make significant improvement.

Central Tendency and Variability

The numbers to the right are call center phone pickup time measurements. The central tendency monitor of average is .0499. It is the balance point of the values and is shown in the chart below.

0.0497	0.0508	0.0506	0.0502
0.0503	0.0509	0.0495	0.0505
0.0490	0.0496	0.0487	0.0497
0.0503	0.0492	0.0497	0.0499
0.0496	0.0510	0.0494	0.0495

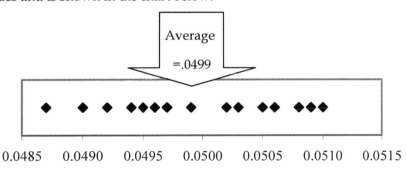

Variability is monitored by range and standard deviation. The chart below shows the range for the phone pickup time measurements.

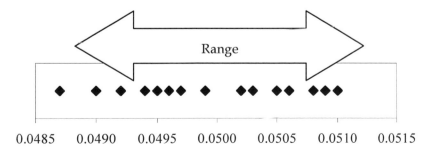

Monitoring Techniques In the Call Center

In the chapter on having it all in our call center, we learned that wait time is a function of processing time average, processing time variability, and agent call utilization. How to monitor two of the wait time drivers has been covered in this chapter. Average monitors the central tendency and standard deviation monitors the variability. This chart shows an average processing time of three minutes and associated standard deviations. One standard deviation is small and the other is larger.

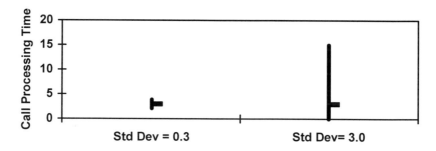

Average Call Processing Time of 3 minutes

Note that 99.8% of calls with the low variation of 0.3 minutes will fall between two and four minutes processing time. The range is derived from a probability calculation. It is important to appreciate the spread of the calls and their impact on wait time.

Also the standard deviation of 99.8% of the calls with the larger variation of 3.0 minutes, will fall between zero and fifteen minutes processing time. This spread will have a large wait time if all the other drivers are kept stable.

This chart shows a third standard deviation of 30 minutes, which is a large amount of variability for an average processing time of 3 minutes.

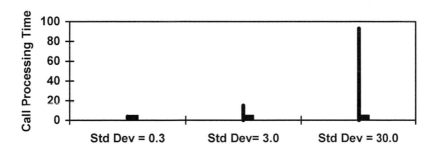

This new larger spread will have between zero and ninety minutes processing time for 99.8% of calls with the larger variation of 3.0 minutes standard deviation. This spread will have a larger wait time if all the other drivers are kept stable.

Now we can apply our metric monitors to the queuing science that we covered in our chapter on "Having it All".

The chart below shows two scenarios, each with an average processing time of 3.0 minutes. One situation is with a low variability of .3 minutes and the other is with a high variability of 30.0 minutes. The high variability situation's wait time increases at a much higher rate than the low variability case.

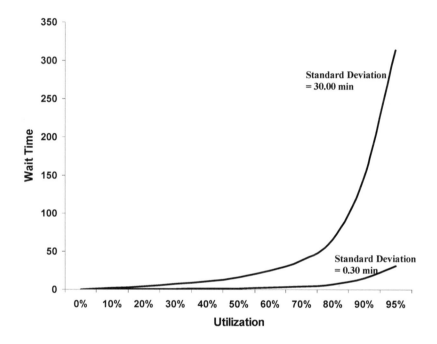

With this knowledge we can attempt to explain the reason for the high variability and then creatively develop express lanes like our grocery store example. This will allow us to reduce cost and reduce wait time together. Processing time variability is a key driver in wait time, and we must be vigilant in monitoring it and creative in reducing it.

Chapter Four:
Metric Dashboard

In the 21st century call centers have radically changed from their beginnings in the early 1900s. Now rather than one simple call center type where everyone does the same thing and every call is about the same length, we have five uniquely different call center types. The five types — routing, notification, call management, processing, and content dissemination--require specialized tools, method, processes, and metrics.

In those early days of the simple call center, the center's largest expenses were far and away telephone service charges. These large and complex phone bills drove management to focus on these telephone charges. Today the science inside the center is more complex because of the many demands from the five different call center types. This requires a conceptual understanding of call center science issues, from express lane determination, to lane balancing, plus the original telephony issues. Metrics play a huge role in the design of an effective call center and the decision-making required to run an optimal call center.

Metrics are the information for running a center. Not having metrics is like an airliner not having gauges like an altimeter. You can fly the plane when the conditions are smooth and clear, but when the plane is in bad weather you are in real trouble. You can have a center with no metrics but you can only run an effective center when you have the information metrics provides.

The airline pilot has a complete complement of gauges on his dashboard describing every aspect of the airplane. Our call center dashboard must also have a complement of metrics telling the complete call center story. To this end, the three Principles of Process Management will assist us to rapidly and proactively respond to the ever-changing business world so that we always have an effective center. These principles are the First Principle of Product and Process, the Second Principle of Division of Labor, and the Third Principle of Walkabout® base-camp.

Why Metrics: Monitoring a Base-camp

The Third Principle of Process Management states *an effective operation must be built on a base of correctness, consistency, and capability. The strategic decision makers provide a correct facility for the tactical decision makers to run correctly. Consistency is the level at which the tactical workforce is able to hit the target. Capability is strategic in nature. It measures the facility's ability to provide what the customer wants.*

Walkabout® Base-camp

Running your call center is like an expedition ascending a mountain to its summit. A mountain climbing expedition always meets roadblocks. The expedition requires certain essential elements to overcome these obstacles and so does running your center. The mountain climbing expedition's essentials include the right equipment, access to the essentials of life (food, water, air), a stable launch point, and properly trained team members. These essentials are referred to as the base-camp for an expedition. In an effective call center, a base-camp will also be required. The operational base-camp's components are correctness, consistency, and capability which we will refer to as the Walkabout® base-camp.

Correctness

The following chart allows us to discuss the first component of correctness. To explain the concept, imagine that we have a small call center with three agents. We have purchased a ticketing system to track our work.

The first agent opens the ticket when the call comes in, processes the call and posts the required information into the system as the call progresses, and at the completion of the call closes the ticket. The second agent feels that using the ticketing system is too much paperwork or in his words is "nonproductive work" so he chooses to never use the system. The third agent processes all the calls and writes the required information on a sheet of paper. Then, at the end of the day, he posts that work into the ticketing system.

If we enlarge this situation to a center with 30 or 100 or 300 agents, we begin to see that we cannot really tell anything about the center. We have no method to see if someone is doing better or worse than everyone else. In other words, there is no correct process and everyone does the best they can.

First, the strategic correctness must be established. A correct, functional organization with clearly defined roles must be determined. A clearly defined product and a detailed method or process must be created. The strategic decision-makers must develop and clearly communicate these correct processes. The strategist will provide a Walkabout® schematic diagram of the method. On each metric a target will be provided.

WALKABOUT™ Dependency Diagram   Area: Call Center

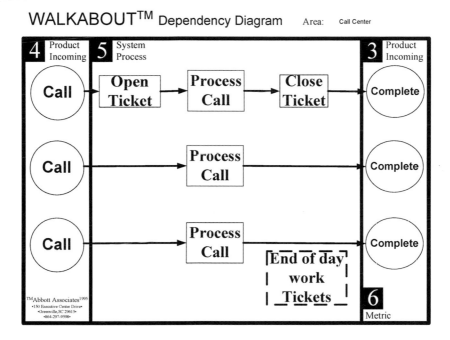

For the center we have been discussing the strategist must first establish a correct method. The strategist decides that whenever a call comes in, a ticket must be opened, then the call will be processed with all information documented during the call, and finally when the call is complete the ticket will be closed. This must be communicated to the tactical workforce.

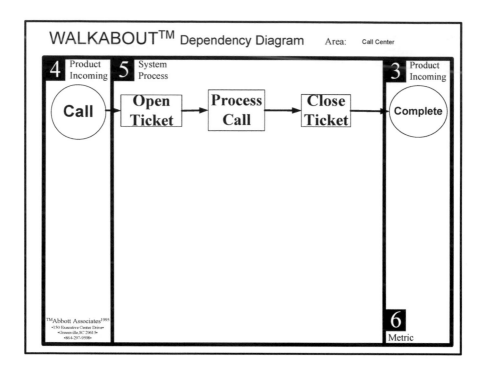

The tactical workforce (our line supervisors and agents) must brilliantly execute the plan, methods, and target settings. Brilliant execution should not be confused with perfection. We, as human beings, will always strive for perfection but the reality is that it may be outside our grasp. Correctness is the first step toward building the Walkabout® base-camp. This correctness is key for our call center metrics to perform properly.

Consistency

The second step toward completing the base-camp means monitoring each call center metric. This will determine how consistent each product and process metric is. As we tacticians strive for perfection, this consistency provides a way of predicting what will be produced time after time. Each metric must have its own consistency established. This consistency is monitored through the use of tactical mathematical tools called control charts. These are our first view of the metrics. These tactical views must be used for running our provided facility.

Capability

Finally the strategic decision-maker is positioned to assess how well the call center meets the customer's expectation. This is the center's capability.

Take special note: Correctly and consistently running the provided facility are tactical issues. Capability is a strategic issue. Both the tactician and strategist must work together with brilliance to achieve the best performance from the center.

What Can We Manage?

Let's clarify the word manage. The dictionary defines **manage** as *exerting control over*. A person can run an operation reacting to the problems of the day, but this is not managing it is simply reacting.

Much discussion is made of monitoring dropped calls. Monitoring dropped calls is interesting but it does not help us know what to manage.

To run a call center optimally, we must understand the First Principle of Process Management. Clearly understanding this principle is mandatory to everything we will do. The First Principle of Process Management states *a fundamental understanding of BOTH the product and process is essential to improvement. Both the product and the process must be described and understood individually and separately. The underlying component for improving the product is the process.*

The First Principle's final sentence is the key. Often all our efforts and energies are directed at analyzing the product. As an example, eating a lot of biscuits does nothing to the baking effort. Having the ability to differentiate between good and bad biscuits does not make you a fine baker. A baker must focus his attention on the baking process. The temperature of the oven, how long the biscuits are in the oven, the location of the baking tray, etc. are the key components for the baker. These are the measures of the process; for the tactician, they are significantly more important than eating the biscuits!

In a call center monitoring dropped call does not help us know how to stop dropped calls. The reason most dropped calls occur is because the caller's wait time is too long. But, without adding queuing science, we can't manage wait time, so what are the process issues that drive wait time. We learned earlier that wait time is a function of processing time average, processing time variability, and utilization. We *can* exert control over call processing time central tendency, variability, and agent utilization. Now we have identified what we can manage. These are critical to managing an effective call center. To manage them we must have process metrics of call processing time central tendency, variability, and agent utilization.

Obviously, the person running the call center must focus their attention on the process, and their knowledge of it must continue to increase. My Grandma told me the only way to learn how to make biscuits was to get into the kitchen and learn about the oven. Similarly, to improve our product, we must understand our process, and this understanding must be converted into a process knowledge base that we can use to improve our product. The only way to get this knowledge is through metrics.

The Importance of Process Data: When we just monitor a product metric like dropped calls, we are aware of its deterioration or improvement only. We might be aware of the change but we do not have a reason for it. Product monitoring is important, but it is reactionary, tolerates waste with no understanding of why, and accepts improvement with no understanding of why.

Without understanding why we cannot operate our call center to its maximum performance. For us to make Grandma's biscuits, we must understand why things occur the way they do. Product information gives no insight into why we made good biscuits or why we burnt the biscuits. Since we don't know why we are making good biscuits, we cannot repeat the activities that produced them. This loss of knowledge is tragic.

When we monitor the process and the product, the process parameters, like agent utilization, allow us to know the conditions that caused the change. Monitoring both the product and the process is essential to proactive decisions, improvements, eliminating waste, reducing cost, and understanding the "whys" of change.

Knowledge of "why" allows us to improve continuously. By adding knowledge about the activities required to make a biscuit (process), we begin to learn what is required to make good biscuits. The information about the different processes that were used for good biscuits and defective biscuits allows us to continue to repeat the improvements and to discontinue the defects.

In the perfect world of my grandmother and her biscuits, I never saw her check the biscuits when she removed them from the oven. She kept her focus on the process. Since she knew all the subtleties of baking, she would take corrective action as the oven was cooking the biscuits so that, in a proactive manner, she avoided ever making any burnt biscuits. She was a perfect chef; unfortunately, most of us are not perfect chefs of our processes.

Since we live in a not-so-perfect world, and our knowledge of our process is not nearly so complete as my grandmother's was about her oven, we must continue to monitor both our biscuits and our oven with equal intensity. More precisely, we must monitor *both* process and product. In our call center some examples of product metrics are dropped calls or the amount of time a customer waits for someone to answer his call. Examples of process metrics are the incoming call volume, average call processing time, call processing time variability, and agent utilization.

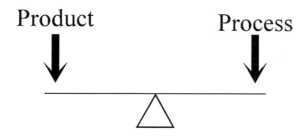

As we gather data, we must accumulate equal amounts of knowledge about the product *and* the process. This will allow us to build a knowledge base for both.

Increased analysis of the product does not equate to increased knowledge of the process. Knowledge of the process and product are two separate but equal efforts and results. Both product and process knowledge is necessary for improvements.

In our call center, monitoring process metrics like agent utilization allows us to become proactive managers.

Using Metrics for Decision-making

The Second Principle of Process Management states that *Division of Labor is the framework for all aspects of decision-making. It must be clearly understood to separate the policy, strategic, and tactical decisions. Operations makes the tactical decisions of running the facility. Management makes the strategic decisions of assessing the facility's suitability for the job. Executives make the policy decisions of providing the vision for the business.*

The Second Principle of Process Management Summarized: Division of Labor drives the decision-making process. It dictates who will be in charge of the different kinds of decisions (strategic or tactical). The following table shows us a summary of division of labor and the three decision types.

	Executive	Management	Operations
Decisions	Policy	Strategic	Tactical
Accountability	Matching our products to customer's need	Finding customers who will buy our products	The correct and consistent running of the facility
Responsibility	Future direction of the business	Providing the facility that will produce what the customer wants	Running the provided facility correctly and consistently
Terms	Vision	Capability	Control
Tools for Decisions	Market research, Financial reports	Strategic views from capability studies, Service Level Agreements	Tactical view from control chart, control limits, targets
Duties	Provide and share the vision	Build a plan and assess the impact of change	Execute the plan and detect change
Functions	Develop a business vision	Provide the resources, time, & place to resolve plan changes	Detect change, Determine cause

Call center personnel typically make either strategic or tactical decisions. Let's take a more in-depth look at them.

Tactics are defined as accomplishing the goal using available means. Control is the major tactical issue associated with operational duties. Operations—the supervisors and agents—make the tactical decisions of running the provided facility.

The strategist must provide this facility. A call center facility is made up of physical and intellectual tools. The physical tools are the computers, phone systems, IVR and call directors, etc. The intellectual tools are the knowledge, science, and metrics of how to run the center. Training for both tool types is required. Capability is the major strategic issue associated with management, customer, and sales concerns. The strategist must provide a capable facility for the tactical workforce.

Tactical execution is required for strategic decisions to be effective. If operations fails to correctly run the facility, no strategy will work. The strategic decision-makers must count on the tactical decision-makers to do their job, for only then can the strategic decisions be effective. Many strategic options are available, but they will work only if the operation runs smoothly.

What not to do is just as important as what to do. Second Principle violations must be understood and avoided in order to effectively make decisions. The Good Trooper Award is given to the supervisor who tries to take the responsibility for strategic decisions. The harder a supervisor works with improper instructions (violating the Second Principle), the poorer the call center results. Quality will continue to degenerate. The better and more conscientious the employee, the worse the situation will become because the person will go to any lengths to carry out those improper directions.

When operations violates the Second Principle on an extremely capable process, the call center will appear less capable than it really is. Instead, we must run the call center to its own personality, as correctly and consistently as possible. We must not be lulled into accepting services that are only as good as the customer wants and allow the process to float below the SLA. A broader discussion of SLA is covered in the chapter about strategic terms.

Chapter Four

Tactical Roles

Running the call center is clearly tactical and the job of the tactical decision-maker. These tactical decisions are:

- Noting when a change in the process and product metrics has occurred.
- Alerting management when a change has occurred so that the strategic decision-maker can assess the impact of the change on the product or the process.
- Finding the cause of a change.
- Working with the strategic decision-maker in deciding what action to take.
- Having the process knowledge to know when and what adjustments are required.

Strategic Roles

Peak efficiency is dependent on the strategist providing a correct and capable facility. Our tactical work force must count on the strategic players to deliver their end of the bargain.

Providing the call center facility is clearly strategic and the job of the strategic decision-maker. These strategic decisions are

- Provide the tools, methods, structure, and technology to meet the policy vision of the executive.
- Assess the impact on the customer or user when a change in the process and product metrics has occurred.
- Dynamically retool the center to meet business changes.

Since strategy and tactics are very different, a different metric view for each seems logical. The tactical view supports the need to detect a change. The strategic view supports the assessment of how well the center is performing, as a function of the customer's needs.

You Can't Do It Alone

Understanding who is responsible for each task is key to a successful organization. If supervisors try taking on every role, they risk not being successful in any role. Violating the Second Principle by compounding the responsibilities of management with those of operations leads to chaotic decision-making. The strategic decision-maker can only ask operations to do what the facility is capable of doing. In this way, we can hold operations accountable for correctly and consistently running the call center facility. Management must never abdicate their strategic responsibility to provide a capable facility.

Throughout this book we have discussed the importance of Division of Labor for decision-making, goal setting, and proper analysis. This Division of Labor clarifies the difference between strategic and tactical issues.

Let's discuss the climate in the Southern region of the United States. This will allow me to explain roles and the trust required for an effective team. During a typical summer, a heat wave engulfs the whole Southern region of the United States. Our strategic decision-maker must select the proper tools to keep us cool.

I remember as a boy trying to stay cool in church. The local mortuary (strategist) supplied hand held fans to everyone in our church. Using those fans never kept us cool. Maybe that is why the mortuary was the supplier; they wanted us to know who to call when we passed away from the heat. Motivation, violent hand motion, and rapid bursts could not overcome the lack of a proper tool to keep us cool. As ineffective as they were, those fans were the best tool at the time.

Later, mechanical fans were introduced but the heat still won the battle. Only when air conditioning came along were the hot summer days manageable. Each of these cooling systems (hand fans, motor fans, and air conditioning) must be run to its maximum potential. Then a fair assessment of each option's efficiency can be made. We expect our strategic decision-makers to continually invent, listen to suggestions, and try new options until ultimately an acceptable solution is devised. This acceptable solution is then built into a capable facility.

Tactical personnel cannot overcome bad strategy nor can strategic personnel overcome bad tactical execution. When strategic and tactical personnel both do their jobs, they form a team. Operations is in deep trouble when management does not do its decision-making job of providing the facility. If the facility (available means) is not capable, we are doomed to having dissatisfied customers and stockholders. If operations does not perform its role of running the facility (available means) correctly and consistently, then how can management assess the impact to the customer? The proper support information must come together to build a finely honed partnership that allows for good, effective, clear decisions.

Let's now discuss in detail the metric dashboard all its components. Our dashboard must provide uniquely different views. One view is for the strategist and the other is for the tactician serving their specific role. These views now are specially designed for each type of decision.

Metric Dashboard

A metric dashboard must tell the story of a complete area. The first component of the dashboard is the Walkabout® that shows the process dependencies, metrics, and metric targets. The following will serve as our example for a metric dashboard. This example is a help desk for a point of sales software product.

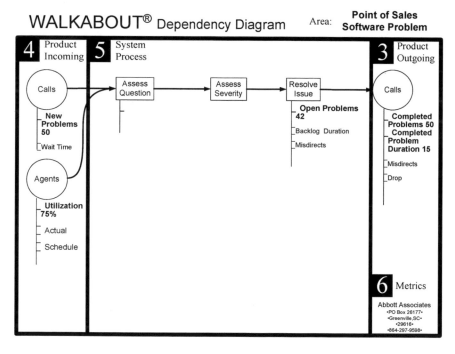

Another option is to purchase a functioning metric dashboard computer system with hot buttons for each metric. The buttons activate a detail presentation for each metric. The first view is the tactical view of consistency, followed by the strategic view of capability.

Walkabout® and Tactical Views

The tactical view is called a control chart. It is the tool to monitor the metrics' consistency around our target. For every metric we must have a control chart monitoring our actual results. We will monitor all three types of metrics: incoming product, process, and outgoing product. To keep our example simple, I have narrowed our discussion to just one metric. The metric that we will use is the number of calls completed.

The control chart gives us a tactical decision-making tool to determine when any movement in our metric measurement of completed calls is truly a change. First the call center was engineered for call volume of 50 calls. We run the call center with this target, gathering and posting the readings. These values will be used to build a time sequence chart.

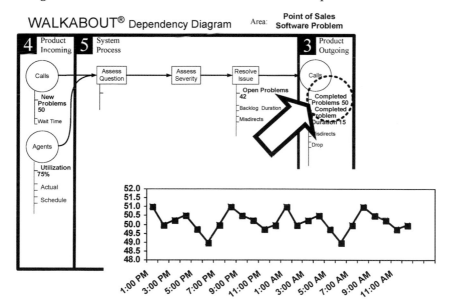

Measurement Frequency

In order to detect patterns, trends, and shifts, we must not only document the time of occurrence but also group the values in chronological sequence to detect the shifts. Chronological sequence is necessary for identifying causes. By maintaining the integrity of the time sequence, we also have the ability to take care of our time-series grouping. The time-series grouping is resolved by using control charts.

The spacing between each subgroup should be the same, if at all possible. The time spacing is called the subgroup frequency. Measurements must not be drawn haphazardly and must not introduce bias toward either good or bad. As nearly as possible, a single subgroup must include readings produced at the same time under the same conditions. In other words, the individuals will be consecutive readings if possible.

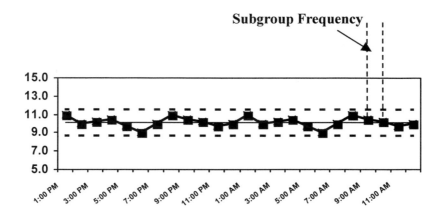

Since our measurement readings are intended to paint a total picture of the call center, they are not just to detect bad service. They must detect change, monitor consistency, and assess impact to the customer.

Subgroup readings will be obtained as frequently as the process demands. As often as the operation changes, readings must be taken. This decision is dictated by the volatility of the operation and not by statistics. For instance, if we wish to detect changes in agent utilization, the frequency may need to be every hour. For a metric like the call volume, a frequency of once per day may serve our needs perfectly.

Some processes are volatile, and change can occur quickly. For these volatile situations the process must be monitored on a very frequent basis. Even if a volatile process is in control, we still need to monitor it frequently to assure that all changes are detected.

Next, based on some math done by our strategic analyst, control limits are calculated from the actual results of running the call center.

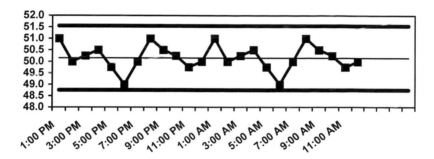

When the metric measurements on the control chart do not violate any of the tactical rules, we can declare our center's metric to be in a state of statistical control. Using the Walkabout® to establish that we are running to the target, we have now passed the first two milestones in our journey to the Walkabout® base camp. Our strategic decision-makers will tackle the third milestone, assessing capability.

The tacticians have kept their end of the bargain. When the center is running correctly and consistently, we are ready for the handoff to the strategist. A true team is built on trust. But we not only trust, we verify. The strategist now takes the measurements and assesses the capability of the center's metrics. This capability shows our actual results compared to the Service Level Agreement (SLA).

The strategist does the capability study by superimposing the actual metric measurements onto the SLA. The chart below is a strategic view called a capability study. The bar reflects the actual measurements showing the number of occurrences by group. The line is the SLA.

The metric measurements from our study are shown with the SLA. When the strategist has done the capability, an expected zero percent defect rate is determined. As long as the process stays correct and consistent with no changes, then we should continue to never see the call volume exceed our abilities.

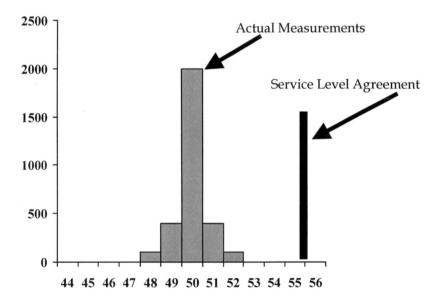

Should you desire to find out the details of control charts and capability studies, the book *Preparing Call Center Metrics* is available through your local or on-line bookstore.

We covered the use of metrics, but let's do a quick review. When a change is detected, the supervisor must do two things. First, a study to determine the cause of the change must be initiated. Second, the supervisor must alert the strategic decision-maker to the change.

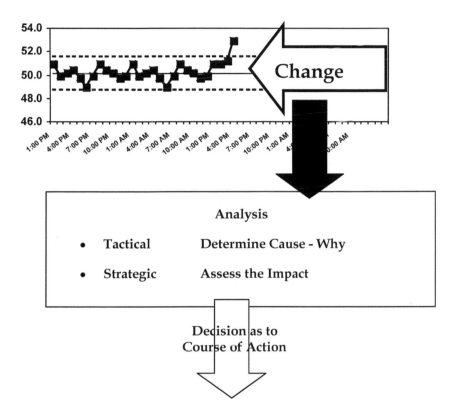

Determining why there was a change is a tactical responsibility. Assessing the impact of the change is a strategic responsibility. The answer to these two questions drives the response to the change. Change must not be confused with defective product or poor service. Change can be either an improving product or a deteriorating product.

The metric dashboard tells the call center story — the Walkabout®, metric hot buttons, tactical views, strategic views, and causal notes.

Effective Managers

Earlier we explained the **Four Traits of an Effective Operation.** Trait one is the ability to respond to rapid change. Trait two is a factored organizational structure supported by defined processes. Trait three is a competent workforce that brilliantly executes the plan. Trait four is optimum decision-making based on proper information. This fourth trait is where metrics play an essential role by providing enough information to make optimal decisions. Metrics support the call center manager.

We also listed the **Four Traits of Effective Managers.**

- They are better at understanding their operation.
- They are better at defining and identifying everyone's roles and responsibilities.
- They are better at assessing the operation for correctness, consistency, and capability on a daily basis.
- They communicate their expectations to the management team so that the team can execute their roles and responsibilities to support the call center manager's goals.

With the Walkabout® metric dashboard, we can master these skills and have an effective call center. Effective call center managers will rapidly understand their facility inside and out, the operational dependencies, and what the key metrics are.

With the metric dashboard the manager has a medium for doing their daily assessment, the Walkabout®. These daily metric reports are from measured metrics not the opinion or voice of the staff. Initially every area of the call center is looked at, and as compliance is achieved, the focus shifts to the change management method. With a base-camp and metrics to test the call center, the manager will be assured that the operation is running correctly, consistently, and capably.

Chapter Five:
Reading the Tactical View

Call Center Change Management

The overall objective of the Walkabout® Method is a correct and consistent call center. The tactician must have tools to detect changes. All tactical views use the same set of alarms to detect these changes. The term "out of control" simply means a change has been detected. The demonstrated effectiveness of a control chart is attributable to its objective and systematic analytical methods. Control charts are tactical tools to detect change in a continuous operation. A series of easy to use and easy to read alarms are provided for the tactician. These alarms are simple but effective.

When a Change Is Real

Often the natural ebb and flow of a process is mistaken for real change. With these false changes, supervisors begin to make unnecessary adjustments. These incorrect adjustments lead to more false change alarms and, thus, more incorrect adjustments.

To prevent that misinterpretation, a set of benchmarks is required to establish what is typical for a particular call center. The control chart's limits provide the means to differentiate between what is typical and what is unusual behavior for a process and product. Remember, what is usual for one center may be bizarre for another. SPC provides the tools to separate the typical from the unusual.

Control charts are comprised of a few simple alarms that note a change is taking place and that an immediate initiation of the causal search should be advanced at full speed.

We are narrowing our scope to focus on the tactical issue of consistency. Data is gathered and each set is immediately tested for a shift. If no shift is detected, no action or adjustments are necessary. Only when a real change is detected is research required. Since our tactician's (supervisor's) time is so precious, he must only research a real change. He must not waste his time researching what is the natural ebb and flow of a process or product. Remember, never take action just because an alarm is noted. The cause must always be found before taking action.

Where the Tactical View Rules Came From

Everyone has been graded on a bell-shaped curve at some point in school. The name for this bell curve is the **normal distribution**. The normal distribution is used to convert the actual grades or test scores to a letter grade.

The normal distribution is symmetric around its average. Fifty percent of the data points are above the average and fifty percent of the measurements are below the average. The frequency of occurrence (or the number of occurrences) drops rapidly as we move further and further away from the center. This characteristic is true both above and below the average. The frequencies of occurrences above and below the average are symmetric as well.

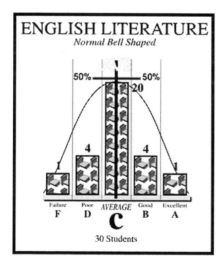

ENGLISH LITERATURE
Normal Bell Shaped
50% — 50%
20
4   4
Failure Poor AVERAGE Good Excellent
F   D   **C**   B   A
30 Students

This graphic shows the spread of grades from an English literature class of thirty students. It shows how a typical class in English literature could have been graded using a bell shaped curve. Out of a class of thirty students twenty would receive a "C", four would receive a "B", another four would receive a "D", one would receive an "A", and one would receive an "F". This would represent a typical class.

All the alarms used by the tactical views are based on the same bell curve that our teachers used in school. Since the alarms are based on the normal distribution, we must follow the calculations derived from the algorithm for control limits.

The call center metrics for each express lane will have alarms calculated on its own past history. These calculated control limits provide the alarms that have the right sensitivity for our unique call center and all its processes. These alarms are called control limits and can tell when a change is real.

These limits require maintenance to assure that they evolve as our center and express lanes change. The limits need to reflect our call center's current state not our hoped for results.

The alarm system is simple but it is always effective in identifying an alarm. The following pages show us what these alarm are. When this tactical tool works with the companion strategic tools we have a powerful comprehensive system for improving and maintaining our call center.

Steps for Finding an Alarm

There is a control chart for variability and another for central tendency. Variability is often skipped, misunderstood, and ignored. I always monitor the variability first, and check central tendency second. Once each component has been monitored for change, I look at both charts together.

To summarize, the three steps are

1. Check Variability
2. Check Central Tendency
3. Check Both – variability and central tendency together

We must always check both variability and central tendency for change. The most common mistake in controlling a process is to test only for shifts in the central tendency, or center; variability must be monitored as well.

The next few pages show the alarms used on a control chart. Remember that these alarms are a simple way to detect change.

Remember – never act on an alarm. All the alarms are alerts that a change has occurred in the process or product. Before any action can be taken, the cause of the alarm must be identified. The control chart does not tell the cause but only alerts us to start an investigation. The quicker the investigation starts, the better our chances that we will determine the cause.

The "Single Point Outside Control Limits" Alarm

Any data point outside the control limits requires investigation because the odds are very remote that a controlled process could produce such a measurement by accident. The chart should trigger an alert to investigate and determine the cause and the impact of the change.

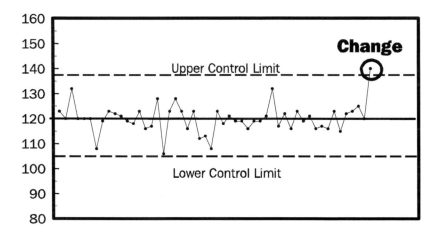

Any point falling outside the chart control limits is an indication that a change is occurring. Any range value falling outside the chart control limits is an indication that variability is changing. An immediate investigation of either situation is required.

The "Series of Points Outside Control Limits" Alarm

Since the odds of a single data point outside the control limits is rare, then a *series* of data points outside the limits must be extremely rare.

The probability of having multiple consecutive data points outside the control limits is low. It would be almost impossible to have four consecutive data points outside the control limits that did not show change. This leads us to the conclusion that this must truly be a shift in the metric that is being monitored. The control chart below shows this particular situation.

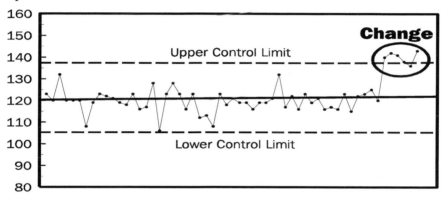

The "Jump in Level" Alarm

Many people mistakenly look only for the alarms that we just covered. Control charts were designed to detect much more subtle changes than those. Because control chart methods are designed to detect minor changes, many of our alarms are based around values that are inside the control limits. These alarms are geared to detect the most minor of shifts for any one particular call center. The first change that is detected with data inside the control limits is a *jump in level*. This particular alarm is geared for minor shifts above the mean of the central tendency.

The alarm is seven consecutive data points above the center point of the control chart, with none of the data points falling outside the control limits. The chart below reflects this particular alarm.

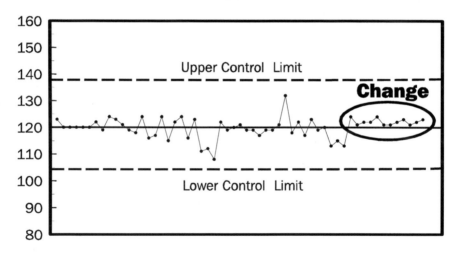

An alarm similar to the above is seven consecutive data points all below the center point of the control chart, but none of the data points outside the control limits.

The first indication of an alarm is when seven consecutive points are on the same side of the centerline but still within the control limits. The more consecutive values on one side of the center, the bigger the alarm.

The "Trend" Alarm

Another minor shift that is important is a *trend*. Trends can take the form of going up or coming down. Once again, minor shifts are what the control chart's detection mechanism looks for. A trend can also be found where the data is inside the control limits.

This particular alarm, illustrated below, is geared to detect a slow shift in a downward direction ("trending down"). It is described as seven consecutive points with each point lower than the last point and no points outside the control limits.

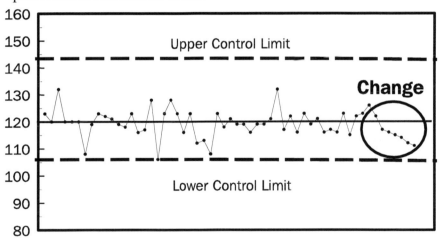

The same idea applies to the reverse, where the trend is increasing. This particular alarm is geared to detect a slow shift in an upward direction ("trending up"). This alarm is seven consecutive points with each point higher than the last point and none of the points outside the control limits.

Keep in mind, control charts must be viewed in a total context of all the information that is available. Just because no control chart alarms have gone off does not mean that other information might not cause an alert.

The "Too Close" Alarm

If the class grades were not spread like the bell-shaped curve of the normal distribution so that every student received a "C", we would immediately conclude that something was wrong in this class. If all the past classes had shown the normal bell-shaped spread and this new class had all "Cs," we could conclude that something about this current class had changed. The too close alarm is analogous to all the students receiving a "C" grade.

The zone one area on a control chart includes 68% of the values and is shown below. If all of the measurement chart postings fall within this zone one (all "Cs"), we can conclude that something about the process has changed. If too many of the values are clustered around the mean, an alarm is indicated. Remember, this is not an indication of bad product or good product, but an indication of change that needs to be investigated.

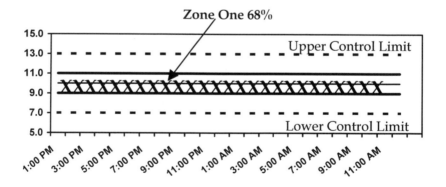

On the control chart below, all the data points are inside the zone one area. This chart is an example of the "too close" alarm going off. This alarm, like all the other alarms, must be investigated immediately.

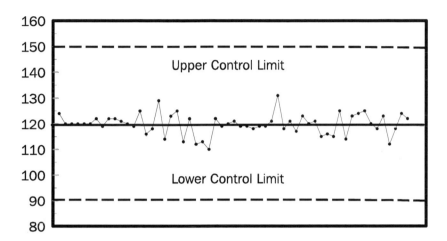

Minor change going unnoticed over time may seem trivial, however these minor changes have a compounding effect. Over time, they allow us to miss major improvement opportunities or slide into major defect problems.

The "Too Far Apart" or "Spread" Alarm

In the properly distributed literature class, four students would be expected to make a "B" and another four students would be expected to make a "D." Zone two on the control chart is like the "B" and "D" of the literature class and includes about 27% of the values.

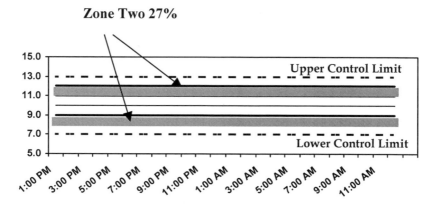

Zone Two 27%

One "A" and one "F" would be expected. Zone three on the control chart is like the "A" and "F" of the literature class and includes about 5% of the values.

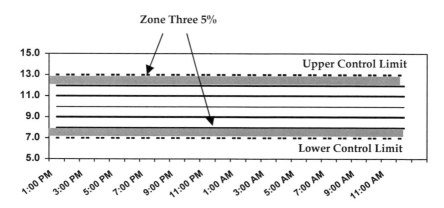

Zone Three 5%

The total number of data points in zones two and three should be 32%. The alarm here is if more than 32% of the data points are in zones two and three. This becomes just as big an alarm as all the prior alarms. If everyone in the literature class got As, Bs, Ds, and Fs, but no Cs, then we would surmise that a change had occurred.

On the control chart below, none of the values fall inside zone one (no "Cs"), but no values are outside the control limits. This is an example of the spread alarm.

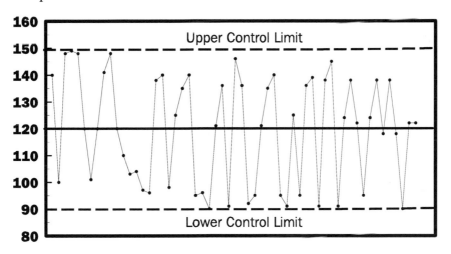

Summary of Interpretation Guidelines

The table below summarizes the alarms that we use to monitor or detect any shifts, patterns, or trends.

- Single point outside the control limits
- A series of points outside the control limits
- Seven consecutive points increasing (or decreasing) from the last point
- Seven consecutive points above (or below) the average
- More than 68% of the points in the first zone
- More than 32% of the points outside the first zone but still within the control limits

Chapter Six:

Tactical Use of Metrics

The tactical view is for the tactical decisions of correct and consistent running of the facility and change management. The tactical view of metrics was never intended to be used as an indication of how well the product, service, or call center meets the customer's needs. Tacticians are responsible for noting when a change, finding the cause of a change, and having the process knowledge to know when and what adjustments are required.

The objective of a tactical view is to help the tactician run the call center consistently. This is referred to as being in control. Because change can be either improvement or deterioration, any change must be identified immediately so that management can assess the impact to the customer. Since the change must be detected quickly, a change detector is critical. That is exactly what the tactical view is.

I hope you have a smoke detector in your house. The smoke detector sits quietly in the background until smoke or fire is detected. When the detector senses these situations, it sounds the call to arms loudly and aggressively. No action is taken based on the alarm alone, but immediate inquiry into the situation is required. We must know the cause of the fire before taking action because if we throw water on a grease fire, the fire will spread. Once the smoke alarm is activated, we immediately search the house to find the cause of the alarm. When the fire's cause is identified, we can make a decision about what to do. This is exactly how the tactical view works--instantly alerting the supervisor to any change and triggering our research as to the cause.

When we are in control, we are running the call center in a steady fashion. In control is another way of saying that the center is running with no change from the center's typical running results. Tactical views show when a change has occurred for a particular process. Timely reporting with a smoke detector is critical. Immediately knowing when a change has occurred in the call center is just as critical.

Conditions and changes in the past cannot be resolved and fixed, but we can act upon the current situation. Tactical view alarms must be reported in a timely manner to allow us the opportunity to determine the reason why the change has occurred. Tactical views demand that all results be posted immediately.

As we know from our coverage of monitoring metrics, two components must be monitored: central tendency and variability. Our tactical views are the ongoing surveillance tools for a continuous process to alert us to any change in these components.

A tactical view displays changes over time. The charts are then analyzed in pairs to monitor central tendency and variability.

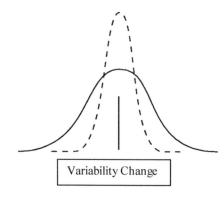

Variability Change

One chart displays changes in the variability of the measurements. The variability can either tighten or spread. The example here shows the variability collapsing. The solid line in this chart shows the original distribution. The dotted curve of our changed process is tightened because of the variability change. This picture depicts the effect of reduced variability.

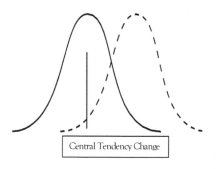

Central Tendency Change

A second chart displays the average values to detect shifts in the central tendency. The solid curve represents the original distribution. The central tendency can shift left or right from its current position. In this example, the center has moved to the right from the current center position. The dotted curve shows the center point of the distribution changing to a higher level.

Shifts in both the central tendency and variability can occur, and each can occur by itself. Tactical views must be able to detect both the central tendency shift and the variability shift. If only one tactical view attempted to detect two simultaneous shifts, the alarm might not draw attention to both areas.

The reason for having two smoke detectors, one in the kitchen and one in the bedroom, is to help reduce the search area for the fire causing the alarm. If the smoke detector in the kitchen is buzzing, then our first investigation is going to be in the kitchen. We can quickly go to the area of the house where the alarm has sounded. Now our fire search is focused in one specific area to determine the cause and what appropriate action will be needed. It is much easier to determine the proper action to take when our efforts have been focused.

In like manner, we always need two tactical views--one to monitor variability and one to monitor central tendency. This, like the multiple smoke detectors, will help us reduce our search and investigation area.

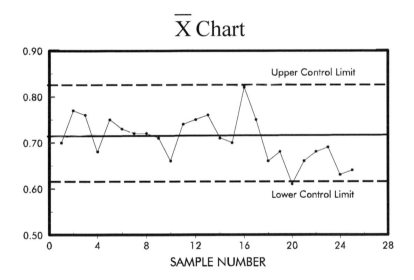

The central tendency chart called X-bar chart is designed to monitor the movement or changes in the central tendency of the process.

The variability chart called R chart is designed to monitor the movement or changes in the variability of the process.

R Chart

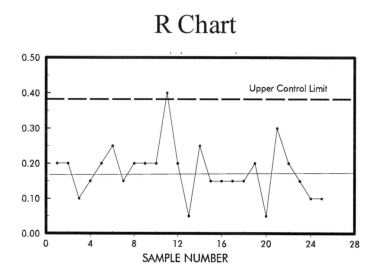

Data is gathered to monitor against the alarm mechanism (control limits) for changes in the conditions of the call center metrics. When an out-of-control situation, or change, is detected, the tactical view has done its job. The following tasks must then be undertaken.

- Investigate the cause
- Alert management to the change so that a strategic assessment of the impact can be made
- Decide what to do

The tactical view component is one player on the decision-making team. A tactical view helps the tactician understand his process and establish how to correctly and consistently run it. The chart also establishes the typical patterns for the process and alerts the tactician to any deviations from the norm. These deviations are "out of control." Many people are confused by the term **out of control** but it simply is another word for change.

If no change is detected, we must wait for the next readings. If a change is detected, our investigation begins to determine the cause and assess the impact. We decide what action to take once all the prior steps are complete. Once a change is detected, we are just at the start of our journey; we must move on to our investigation efforts.

The alarm is a change detection mechanism. These process or product metric changes are outside the typical behavior of the call center. Remember that change can be either improvement or deterioration. For progress (improvement) to be made, change has to occur.

The tactical view is the tool to identify when the change warrants investigation. Our investigation is an attempt to determine the reason the change took place. This is referred to as finding the cause. As we find the cause or causes our knowledge will grow, and with knowledge comes improvement.

In many ways the tactical view (when used in conjunction with strategic tools) is our improvement detector. Actually the tactical view can only find change, but without the tactical view, change may go unnoticed. This is particularly true of minor change. Over time, many small, minor changes will accumulate to major change.

Once a change has been documented as more than just a fluke, the tactical role becomes even more focused on the correct and consistent running of the call center. The tactician must now focus on what caused the change while the strategic focus is to assess the impact.

Initiate Investigation

Our investigation is composed of two parts: one tactical and one strategic. A clear understanding of the roles of both the strategic and tactical players is key. Once the individual roles are clear, the players must function together as a team for effective action.

The tactical decision-makers begin investigating to determine the cause of the alarm. These causes will increase our understanding of the process and product. This knowledge is crucial for improvement. Once the knowledge has been learned, it must be retained and shared with all associates. The tacticians must also alert the strategic decision-makers that a change has occurred so that an assessment of the impact of the change can be made.

The strategic decision-makers must simultaneously (while the cause is being investigated) assess the impact of product or process change on the customer.

Once the cause has been identified and the capability determined, a course of action must be chosen. This is a team decision by both the strategic and tactical decision-makers.

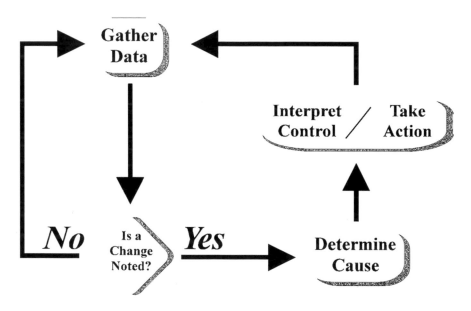

The above chart depicts the steps to action based on a tactical view alarm. We regularly gather data and test for change. If no change is detected, then the tactician continues his work until the next reading is taken. If a change is detected, the tactician begins the research for determining the cause of the change. After the cause of the change is determined, we are ready to begin the decision of how to act.

Remember, never take action just because an alarm is noted. The cause must be identified before any action is taken.

What Are Causes?

Knowledge base linking is the attempt to determine what caused something to happen. Effects are the things that happened. Deducing what caused the effect is the most difficult task we will encounter. Since all of the facts are never known, determining the cause of an effect is often difficult. True cause identification is an ongoing effort. We will continually add to our true causes, and in doing so, we will increase our knowledge base.

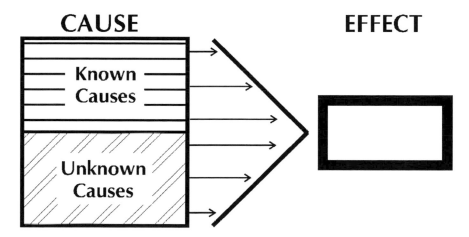

Since we never know all the facts or have a complete picture, we must continually review our determinations and findings. We must never view our findings as laws or standards that cannot be improved. The disparity of known causes directly impacts our determinations and is due to a lack of all the facts or a failure to understand the meaning of the facts we have. The magnitude of this disparity must be continually investigated.

We first think of the call center designer, product designer, or process engineer as the most likely candidate to determine the cause of a change. These individuals are well equipped with technical skills. However the investigation process must begin quickly so that the causal identification trail does not get cold. The problem with all the people listed is that their timely availability is questionable. Engineers, management, and designers are strategic and must be involved in the final action plan.

Change happens at all times of the day, weekends, holidays, and even at 3:00 AM on Saturday. Since our efforts must occur immediately, the person closest to the call center operation must be the causal searcher. This narrows our scope to the prime person most familiar with the call center - the supervisor. The supervisor, our tactician, will lead the efforts to finding the cause of the change.

All the technical resources that can support the supervisor must be brought into play to find the cause. As the supervisor finds these causes, the knowledge base about the process and product will be increased.

Our objective is to continually reduce this disparity and achieve total knowledge of the true causes. Over time we must strive to increase our knowledge base.

Metrics and Science

Effects are rarely the result of a single simple cause. Since most causes are seldom known, we should expect gaps in our knowledge base. These gaps of knowledge should keep us alert to the fact that effects are not always the result of known causes. Serious trouble will be encountered if the facts are forcibly stretched to explain the effect. A wise person is one who appreciates his lack of total knowledge.

To build our total knowledge base, our analysis must be based only on a historical record and science. This allows us to begin causal linking. This will not preclude our adding knowledge of changes in the future to better understand the cause. This is like driving a car. We look through the rear view mirror to understand where we have been. This view also allows us to see cars coming from the rear. We look through the front windshield to understand things coming up such as a curve in the road or a car on our side of the street.

The data for our analysis must begin at the basic element. Our analysis must begin both from the bottom and from the top, allowing the art of causal analysis to take place.

Causal linking is easy when we view the most immediate occurrence that is known. The further removed the causes are from the effect, the more difficult the linking task. This linking must track the links of the chain from process to product. All products and processes are interrelated. This interrelationship impacts the outcome (effect).

To better understand the investigation and analysis that will be required, let's define the type of causes that can come into play.

Assignable Causes

As we begin to study our information, a clear understanding of what a cause means and the types of causes which are possible is crucial to understanding what actions are required. We must first understand that we are looking for change. Change includes both improvement and deterioration. We must understand which type of change we are dealing with in order to understand our courses of action.

The dictionary defines **assign** as *to set aside or give out in portions or shares.* **Cause** is defined as *the one, such as a person, an event, or a condition, that is responsible for an action or a result.* When we put the dictionary's definitions into action, we conclude that **assignable causes** are those that definitely result in a particular effect. As we read the definitions, we see that all causes do not have equal impact.

As we increase our knowledge base, we must strive to include all causes no matter how small their impact. A series of minor causes can lead to a cumulative impact that is very large. Too often we are only looking for the Big Bang. We are searching for both major and minor causes, so that we can build our knowledge base to be all-inclusive.

Causes are neither good nor bad but simply a statement of fact. A cause is why something happened or changed. For us to make improvements, we must first detect change and then determine its cause. We will diligently search for all causes, both those bringing about improvement and those resulting in deterioration. This information will allow us to increase our knowledge base of the process.

The reason causes are so important is that they give us the information to know what will happen in a particular situation. Many times an associate who has been on the job for years will still not know the cause of an adjustment. There is a major difference between thirty years on the job and thirty years of experience. With thirty years of experience, we

99

have built a huge knowledge base that will tell us what is going to happen to the process.

Types of Assignable Causes

For us to effectively make a decision, to understand its impact, and to know the correct type of decision, we must know what type of cause is involved. There are three kinds of causes: 1) special, 2) common, and 3) tampering. Sometimes no cause is found.

Special causes are causes within one's control. The person running the call center is directly involved in the creation of a special cause. Special causes are isolated to one particular process and impact only that one process. As I drive down the street, the car's course adjustments are caused by my movement of the steering wheel. My pressure on the accelerator determines the car's speed.

In the same way, only a supervisor in the center can make adjustments to his process. These could include script changes or the number of agents in use. No matter how the agent might desire these settings to impact other areas of the center, it's pretty obvious that these changes, like the car's course adjustments, will have no effect on other areas.

Since special causes are local in nature (assigned to the driver or the supervisor), local action is required to resolve them. The supervisor must resolve the effects by dealing with the cause locally.

Special causes are the supervisor's responsibility for resolution. Local actions are usually required to eliminate these special causes and can usually be taken by people close to the process. Tactical decisions and tactical actions are generally used to deal with special causes. The driver of the car above must make course corrections to assure the safe driving of the vehicle. Such corrections are tactical decisions.

Common causes are causes outside one's control. These influences generally occur across the board for all processes, thus the name common. The supervisor is usually not the generator of common causes. If the call volume increases in an IT help desk because a new version of software has been released, the supervisor is not involved in this cause of change. Common causes are things that have global impact across the group. Common causes impact the whole center, and the impact is similar on all involved. Using the driving example, I might choose to slow the speed of my car on a rainy day. This adjustment to my speed is caused by the rain, which is outside my control. Most other drivers would also slow down due to the bad weather conditions. All the cars are being impacted by the weather, and weather is common to all. No action by the drivers, either singularly or together, could change the weather.

Since common causes are outside local control, outside sources must resolve these causes. Generally this is thought of as a managerial issue, because management has overall control of the facility, and the actions on the system almost always require management action for correction. Strategic decisions and strategic actions are generally used to resolve common causes. For example, if the software release has caused an increase in call volume that we anticipate will stay for a long period of time, the call center director must make strategic decisions to resolve the problem with additional staff or strategically decide to accept the longer wait times. No amount of tactical action can resolve this problem.

Tampering causes are changes that are caused by too much control. Tampering occurs when we are trying to take action on something that should not be changed. This is typically caused by our failure to understand and comprehend the Second Principle of Process Management. Remember, Division of Labor is the framework for all aspects of decision-making. Tampering occurs when a tactician tries to make strategic decisions like trying to force agents to deviate from their script and abruptly get off the phone to reduce the wait time, or increasing the number of calls processed. A strategist doing the tactician's job violates the Division of Labor. These violations are the reason for most tampering causes.

We must research the many questions surrounding the chain of events that caused an effect. The art of causal analysis and linking is determining which of these questions warrant an investment of the time and money required for further research. In many ways the research is like wildcatting for oil. Many causes will be confirmed. Many causes will be rejected. Often the research leads to more questions. The objective is to continue to build our knowledge base. This information can actually become a bigger asset than the manufacturing facility!

If no cause is found, our challenge is to continually search for the cause. This situation will occur many times, but perseverance is essential to this effort. In my boyhood television days, the "Superman" episodes always talked about a never-ending search for "truth, justice, and the American way." Our search for causes must be like Superman searching for the criminal: a never-ending search for the cause of our change.

Good Tools Misused

Some companies are frustrated because they never see improvements from their metric measurements. They wonder why metrics has failed. Actually, the answer lies in the way they use metrics. A reactionary approach means that we begin our causal research after our product control charts have detected a problem. Metrics were designed to use both product and process control charts in a proactive manner to detect change *before* problems occur.

For an example I will use a center that provides technical support. The example's business is a point of sale software product that is sold to retail stores. The center provides technical support and problem resolution to clients who have purchased the company's point of sale software. Since calling customers may be in the middle of a transaction with their own customer, and have questions or problems, the center's rapid response is critical. This center functions as one of the company's storefronts. We want every call to end with a happy and satisfied caller so our customers want to continue to buy our products.

Dropped Calls

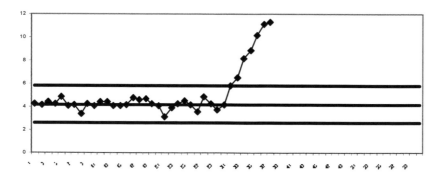

The chart above shows the center's number of dropped calls occurring each day.

If we focus on a product metric like the number of dropped calls, by the time we realize that a shift has occurred we really have a crisis on our hands. We are in damage control mode, fighting fires, and reacting to the problem of the day. Nothing proactive can happen. To make matters worse, we have no way of determining the cause of the dropped calls.

Since our center is a storefront, we want to assure that we keep the dropped calls to a minimum. The main reason that callers drop is because they have grown impatient with our excessive wait time. Below we have our process defined and the metric blueprint for the center.

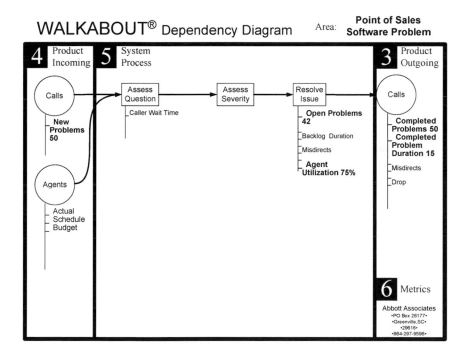

Think about the product metric of dropped calls. A second metric, and a better metric, would be to track the call wait time.

The tactical view below shows the wait increasing. As the wait time increases we would expect our number of dropped calls to increase. If we look at both the wait time metric and the dropped call metric, we see these two metrics track together. In other words, as the wait time increases, the number of dropped calls increases. Also, as the wait time drops, the number of dropped calls falls.

Wait Time

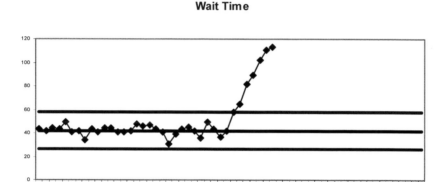

This wait time and dropped call relationship is helpful and interesting, but unless we add science, we cannot manage either dropped calls or wait time. We must have a comprehensive understanding of queuing science, the metric blueprint, and metrics. With this understanding we know what we can manage and what impact they have. We have a true cause and effect understanding of the call center.

Total Picture Working Together

We will use all the metrics plus the Walkabout® below to find the cause and get to the root.

Earlier in the book we covered queuing science. We know that wait time is a function of utilization of the clerk, processing time average, and the processing time variability. The chart below shows the metric blueprint, process, and tactical metric view. The metric views that are shown are wait time, incoming calls, and average processing time. An actual metric dashboard would show all the metrics, but this is enough to explain the concept.

Wait time could increase because our calls are taking longer or because we have a large volume of incoming calls.

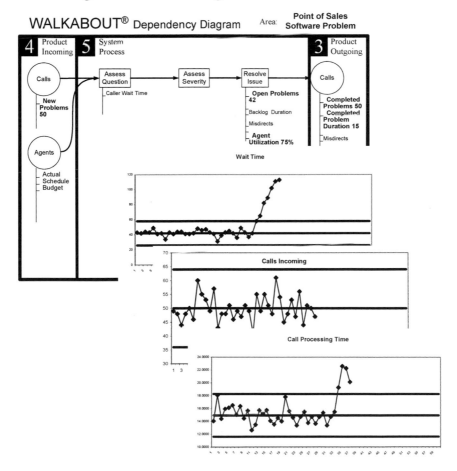

Our metrics show the wait time has increased because the average call processing time has increased. The call volume has remained consistent. With this knowledge we can make a decision regarding a course of action. Some of the actions could be to increase the staff to compensate for the extra time, allow the waits to remain long, and so on.

The queuing science metrics and Walkabout® allows us to proactively manage our center. The issues that allow us to have it all are the processing time average and variability. Call variation has now become a major issue.

In today's world there are five call center types--routing, notification, call management, processing, and content dissemination. Science and metrics allows us to determine what could form a call center express lane. These call center express lanes keep our wait times down, reduce our cost, and provide better performance in our responses to our customers or users. First lets revisit how variability plays a significant role in a modern call center design.

Our grocery store checkout example shows the impact of the drivers of wait time. The graph below, based on the Pollaczek-Kyntchin equation, allows us see all three issues to calculate wait time. In your call center wait time is a function of agent utilization, call processing time average, and call processing time variability.

Since variability has become a major issue every metric must monitor both central tendency and variability.

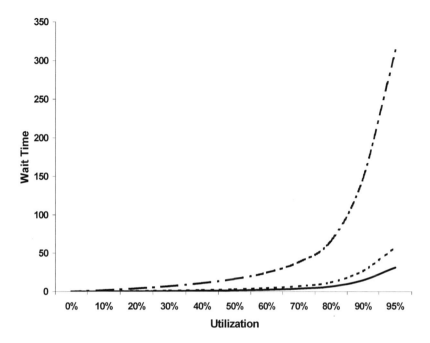

The tactical view below show the monitors of the central tendency and variability for call processing time.

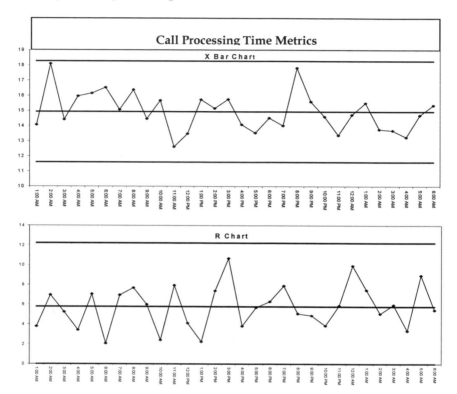

The tactical issues and tactical decisions we covered earlier are listed below:

- Noting when changes in the process and product metrics have occurred.
- Alerting management when a change has occurred so that the strategic decision-maker can assess the impact of the change on the product or the process.
- Finding the cause of a change.
- Working with the strategic decision-maker in deciding what action to take.
- Having the process knowledge to know when and what adjustments are required.

Now we have the total and comprehensive package of tools that allows our tactical workforce to effectively do their role.

Chapter Seven:
Strategic Terms

Division of Labor, as defined in the second principle, drives the decision-making process. Division of Labor is the framework for all aspects of decision-making. It must be clearly understood to separate policy, strategic, and tactical decisions. Operations make the tactical decisions of running the facility. Management makes the strategic decisions of assessing the facility's suitability for the job. Executives make the policy decisions of providing the vision for the business.

Decision-making is defined as reaching a conclusion. For our purposes, the definition must be broadened. We will define a **decision** as *reaching a conclusion plus the **execution** of the decision to reach that conclusion.* Just having a good idea or knowing how to fix a problem is not enough. To say that we have made a decision, we must bring the concept, idea, or solution to completion.

Strategy is defined in the dictionary *as the art of devising or employing plans or stratagems toward a goal.* Strategic decisions assess impact when a change occurs. The strategic decision-maker selects, assesses, and provides the means. All strategic decisions must provide the facility to support the policy vision of the executives.

Strategic decision-makers pick the time, place, and resources that will be used to accomplish the policy vision. Strategy must drive and work in harmony with both policy and tactics. If they get out of balance, all will suffer. Strategic decisions determine the time, place, and resources required for action by our tactician. Patience is required to assure that proper timing and location are determined. Strategic decisions are marked by bold and decisive efforts.

The strategic decision-maker's role is to build a plan and provide the proper resources in a timely manner, and at the right place, to afford the tactical team a successful effort. The strategic decision-maker will also assess changes to the plan to determine impact to the customer.

Simply put, the strategist must provide the facility (time, place, and resources) that will meet the objective. In an operational context, our objective is providing a facility that will make what the customer wants. Now lets dig deeper into strategy by focusing on the customer.

Customer's Perspective

Customer is defined in the dictionary as the person who gives us money for our products or services. The strategist must convert the customer's vision into a tangible product or service and then build a facility that can produce it. To appreciate our customer's perspective so that we can build a facility we must understand our customer.

Since airline travel is part of my regular duties, let's use one of my trips from Greenville, South Carolina, to Denver, Colorado, as an example of perspective. Imagine sitting on the plane ready to take off when the pilot says that we are going not to Denver International Airport (DIA) but instead to somewhere around Denver. He goes on to explain that enroute he will make a decision as to where to land. He explains that to add a little spice to the flight, we may land at the old airport (Stapleton), or possibly at the Boulder, Colorado airport, or possibly at the original destination of Denver International.

Thankfully, this did not really happen, but think about the consequences of such behavior. Passengers would miss their connecting flights, rental agencies would not know where to leave their cars, and other people meeting the passengers would be at a complete loss as to where to find them. A better way must be developed. Just as a pilot must file a clear flight plan and stick to it, we, too, must know where we're headed.

Clarity of purpose is key and two fundamental issues must be addressed. *What does the customer really want? What can and will the customer tolerate today?* Let's look at these separately first.

Customer's Wants

What does the customer want? When a customer purchases our product or uses our service, he normally has a specific purpose in mind. Therefore one of our biggest challenges is to understand the customer's purpose and to assure that we always keep this purpose in mind.

When we are traveling on an airline, our objective is to arrive in Denver, Colorado. When we go to the store for a gallon of milk, we want precisely one gallon. When a half-inch hole is drilled, we want the hole to be exactly a half-inch. For clarity of purpose, our target or definition of "perfect" must be clearly identified. The target must be explicitly defined, and a value for the target must be established.

The product produced by a manufacturing facility must work. When we turn on our car it is easy to see if the motor is working. For a departing commercial airliner the target is the exact stated time. A departure that is early will leave potential customers on the ground and a late departure may mean misconnections. As we move into the service industry, the product of our labors is often clouded as to what perfection would be.

In a call center, what is the target for when we pick up a call and how long we make the customer wait on hold? Since the target is perfection, then no wait time is perfection. Whether we can or even desire to achieve perfection is another issue, but to make strategic decisions we must know what perfection is, as stated by the target.

Knowledge of the target is key to both the customer and our business. How can a plant, operation, or service ever achieve perfection if we do not know what perfect is? Worse yet, if we fail to communicate what perfect is, how can we ever expect to achieve perfection?

Most customers do not demand perfection, but want us continually striving to achieve it. Really though, in their heart of hearts, they do want a perfect product or service. Perfect in quality, with a low price, and no waiting. This leads to our second issue -- how patient are our customers?

Customer Patience

How much patience do our customers have when we ship or deliver bad products and services? What will the customer tolerate today? Tolerances are what the customer will tolerate today or how much leeway from the target will be tolerated today. Another way of asking this is, how far removed from our target can we get before our customers go to someone else? Also, our customer's patience, or tolerance, most likely will decrease over time.

To clarify the idea that patience and tolerances will change, let's visit the grocery store to purchase a gallon of milk.

In the early 1900s when milk was obtained in the barn from Bessy the Cow, the level of tolerance was broad. One day Bessy might deliver four quarts, the next six quarts, and the next none. Our intent, target, or perfection was always to obtain a gallon of milk, but in 1900 customers were much more patient or lenient with Bessy because she delivered all that she could.

What Bessy could and would deliver dictated the amount of incompetence that was acceptable in 1900. We were patient with Bessy, but patience is like shifting sand. Over the years the amount of incompetence that is tolerated (the "tolerance") will decrease. Some times technology delivers these improvements but many differing approaches are available to the strategist. When dairy plants began to bottle milk the tolerance became smaller. Do not be misled that the customers will pay us more for these improvements--they will actually expect the cost and price to come down. In this example, the performance, cost, and delivery time to the customer, will improve over time. In 1990 everything about dairy products was better than in 1900 and our customers' tolerance, or tolerance for incompetence, was much lower in 1990 than in 1900. As the product has gotten better note also that the price has dropped.

What is merely acceptable is very different from the target. First, the customer's perception is multifaceted. What the customer wants is the target or perfection. Tolerance is the amount of patience the customer has with our inability or incompetence to provide a perfect product. Finally, the combination of target and tolerance is the spot at which our product or service is unacceptable. This unacceptable spot is called the specification limits. The service industry and, specifically call centers, help desks, claims center, and customer service centers, use a different term for specification limit called Service Level Agreements (SLA). SLAs are wonderful strategic terms for defining the one dimension of the customer's patience level.

We use the degree of incompetence to explain specification limits. We should not be surprised to see the customer's expectation or target fixed. We should also not be surprised to see the specification limits continually changing. The tolerances are continually changing and getting tighter to drive toward the real expectations of the target: perfection. As the tolerances get tighter, so do the specification limits or the spot where the product becomes unacceptable.

This drawing demonstrates how specification limits will change over time until ultimately customers receive exactly what they want: Perfection!

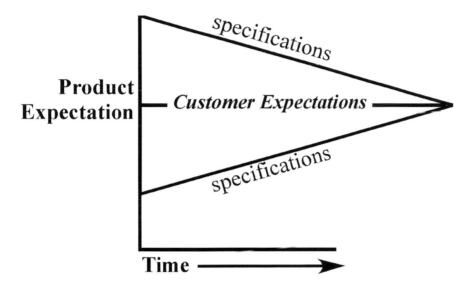

The strategic decision-makers must define the target, tolerances, and the specification limits. At no time should the tactician attempt to independently change these criteria. Any attempts for the tactician to take on the role of the strategist can lead to disaster.

Today, with milk in plastic and cardboard containers at the grocery store, our level of incompetence has shrunk. The target is still one gallon, but now the specification limits are almost exactly one gallon. Notice that over time, the incompetence index of the specification limits will shrink. Also, this must be done without increasing the price.

Specification limits are requirements by our customers or management. They are a measurement attempting to assess the usability of our product. **Specification limits** are defined as *the points at which the product will not be useable by the customer.* Simply having a product that meets the specification limits is not a guarantee of a satisfied customer. This can lead us to a "just good enough" attitude.

The Just Good Enough Trap

Over time we must move toward the target, or the consequences will be severe. For the grocery store example, we must close in on one gallon or risk having to always provide more than the customer's expected amount. The option of giving more than a gallon in order to definitely provide a gallon destroys our cost dimension. Remember our definition of quality: performance, cost, and time are of equal merit. Never allow one dimension to get out of balance with the other two dimensions.

For clarity of purpose, our target must be clearly identified. The target must be explicitly defined, and a value for the target must be established. This target value is a strategic decision. The **target** is *the value that the customer expects should be perfect.*

The specification limits range can only tell us when a call is unacceptable. This range cannot be used for operational purposes. Trying to use this specification range will lead us to poor productivity, inefficient operations, and poorer quality. Operations using this range can create the false sense that the center is running optimally or that we are doing well. This kind of tactical decision-making heads us straight to the *just good enough* philosophy of running the department, service, call center, or facility.

Incorrectly using the specification limits with the entire range as an operational tool allows the sense that we are meeting the customer's expectation and never grasping the bigger issues that we could have exceeded the customer's expectation, or that we are running just below the level where our product or service becomes unacceptable.

Many operations are run to the specification limits' extremes with no thought to customer expectation, targets, perfection, or the future. We rationalize our operational ineffectiveness. As the customer's patience lessens, our ability to exceed their minimal criteria may not be successful. Suddenly the product that we have been providing is no longer acceptable. We then ask ourselves, "Why have our customers changed?" Our customers haven't changed, but we failed to understand all their issues. One issue is their idea of perfection and the second is how much tolerance they have today for our inability to provide perfection. Remember that our customer's tolerance will change and always move in the direction of the target.

The service sector is even more confusing. The service sector product is clouded as to what perfection would be. We attempt to take the two issues of perfection and tolerance and try to use one term, Service Level Agreements, to support both issues. This burden has made many SLAs completely counterproductive. The service level agreement is really a special case of the specification limits.

A **Service Level Agreement** (SLA) is the term for *a specification limit in the service industry and particularly in the call center arena. The SLA is the spot at which the product, process, or service is unacceptable to the customer.* As an example, having call duration times that exceeds our SLA would be unacceptable to our customers. Once again, being within our SLA must not be confused with perfection.

For a call center, we must communicate both the target and the spot at which our service is unacceptable. As an example, when we pick up a call, and how long we make the customer wait on hold, are important metrics. Since the target is perfection, then no wait time is perfection. Whether we can or even desire to achieve perfection is another issue, but to make strategic decisions we must know what perfection is as stated by the target. The spot at which the caller gives up and disconnects the call with no service is the spot at which our service is totally unacceptable. This spot is the specification limit or SLA. If we run our call center at or near the SLA, we put our operation in jeopardy. We are in jeopardy because all our competitors have to do is a slight improvement and they can win over our customers when our customer's patience is exhausted.

Communicating All the Issues

So far, our customer's perspective has been discussed as if the customer will specifically tell us what the product should be like (the targets and tolerances). Many times the customer cannot communicate them. This occurs for a variety of reasons. So all organizations need a customer advocate who will act as the customers' spokesperson. Engineering or design normally does this function.

Engineering product or service design must convert the customer perspective or the product vision into a product design. This design must be detailed into exact criteria for our product. These product criteria must include every aspect of the product. These are referred to as metrics. Metrics are the study areas for the product. This defining phase for the product includes spelling out each metric's target and tolerance. From the metric target and tolerances, the specification limits or SLAs are developed.

Our design group is converting the product vision into a detailed product definition that will meet the needs of the customer.

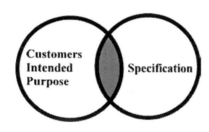

Many times, product specification limits are a simulated test of when the product will not perform the customer's intended purpose. Care must be taken to assure a good overlap between the intended purpose and the specification. Frustrating consequences are caused for the customer and the supplier when we encounter the situation shown in the drawing and the good overlap does not exist.

The drawing depicts the specifications no longer suiting the customer's intended purpose. Over time, we should not be surprised to find our customer's wants and needs changing. Nor should we be surprised that the specification no longer represents the customer's needs. We must always be vigilant to assure that our specifications represent what he needs and wants.

This now leads us to computing the specification. We add the plus tolerance to the target to compute the upper specification limit. The minus tolerance is subtracted from the target to compute the lower specification limit. We add the plus tolerance to the target to compute the SLA.

The following equations compute specification limits:

$$\text{Specification Limits} = \text{Target} \pm \text{Tolerance}$$
$$\text{Specification Limits} = \text{SLA}$$
$$\text{SLA} = \text{Target} + \text{Tolerance}$$

The SLA is used to communicate our requirements. The specification limits and SLAs are used in capability studies. These are defined as the location where the product or process is unusable. The specification limits define where the product or process does not meet the minimum functional requirement. Specification limits and SLAs must be defined for both product and process metrics. Values outside the limits are totally unacceptable.

Let's refine this a bit with some call center examples—a 911 emergency center, a mail order customer sales center, an IT help desk, and a insurance claims center. As we revisit our pick up time, all customers do not have the same patience level. Our target or perfection is pretty much the same for all these examples, but the patience level will vary dramatically.

A 911 emergency call center deals with crises. Any call could be a life and death situation, but the next could just be a routine dispatch for a fender bender. Since each call may be critical, minutes and seconds are crucial to saving a life or stopping a burglar. The level of patience for pick up time must be small; the tolerance might be a pick up of less than four rings.

A mail order business has sales call centers to process customer orders. A sales call center is not a life or death situation but the business has spent large direct mail advertising dollars to attract customers. Any customer that drops because of a frustrating wait is money out of our pocket. Our service tolerance might be less than a minute since this is not only lost revenue, but also we paid money to get the customers to call us.

An IT help desk answers users' questions. The users really have limited recourse, so their tolerance is set because they either wait or they get no answer. These callers patience might be a wait of three minutes.

In an insurance claims center the customers must wait because they truly have no options. They have had an accident and they need their claim processed so that they can be reimbursed. They must wait on our center and have no option right now. When their policy is up for renewal, they might choose another insurance carrier. Since the caller has no options right now and we both know it, they must wait. They might tolerate waits of 30 minutes. Be careful in setting this type of SLA because what we can get away with today may cause us irrevocable damage for future business.

Since each situation and business is different, we are not surprised to find differing service levels. The following recaps our call center examples.

Center Type	SLA
911 emergency calls	4 rings
Mail order house sales	1 minute
IT help desk	3 minutes
Insurance claims	30 minutes

You must set your tolerance, specification limits, and SLAs to your particular business and the patience level of your customers.

Broadening to Include Process

Many people fail to understand the First Principle of Process Management. The first principle reads, *A fundamental understanding of both the product and process is essential to improvement. Both the product and process must be described and understood individually and separately. The underlying component for improving the product is the process.* This last sentence requires that our strategic engineering design not only include product design but also the design of the process.

A process is the specific activities of how we will make the product or deliver the service. Just like the product, each process metric must have a defined target, tolerances, specification limits, and SLAs.

The process metric target is not perfection to the customer but perfect as to how we will make the product. The process tolerance is the amount of leeway that we have in the process while still achieving a passable product or service. The process tolerance should not be used as an operational tool.

The process target and tolerance are used to compute the process specification limits. The process specification or process SLA tells the spot at which our process is not functioning properly and must be shut down. The process tolerance should not be used as an operational tool but as a tool to show when our process metric cannot achieve the desired result. Restated, the process tolerance is the spot at which the process is totally unacceptable.

How we communicate our requirements and needs must be clear to all. Our audience includes both strategic and tactical associates, vendors, and customers. This communication is best accomplished by stating the true target value. With this number stated, the amount of incompetence is expressed through the use of the plus and minus tolerances.

Using a candy example, the target weight is 50 grams. The amount of incompetence that we will tolerate is plus or minus 5 grams. Our specification limits are 55 grams and 45 grams. The lower specification limit protects our customer from being shorted. The upper specification protects the company and stockholder from giving away too much product. If we give away too much product, we will go bankrupt. In a way, this also protects the customer because our bankruptcy would make the product unavailable to the customer.

Our candy process will have conveyor speed and chocolate spray amounts. These will also need targets, tolerances, specification limits, and SLAs. Now we can assess the complete facility by analyzing both the product and the process to give a complete picture of our facility.

Strategic Assessment

The strategist must assess our facility's performance. This assessment is called a capability study.

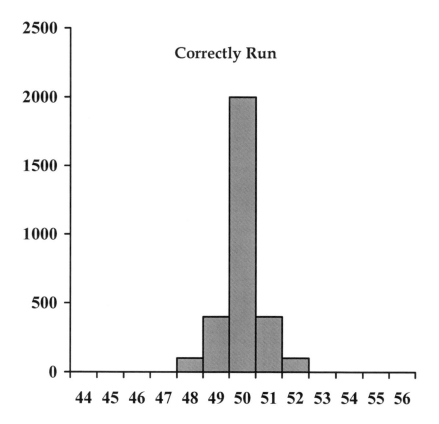

Capability studies paint the picture of what we are making or how the process is performing. This must be done on a process that is run correctly and consistently. A facility's performance assessment, called a capability study, is done on all product and process metrics. This picture is an example of a capability study.

Now we move forward to superimpose the customer requirements onto the picture of our facility.

Specification limits can be expressed as product that is defective only above a certain point, only below a certain point, or outside two measurement points. We may only be concerned with defects on the low side like providing a candy that is too light. We may also be concerned only with defects on the high side like making callers wait too long. Finally, we may be concerned with both high and low defects, like when drilling a hole (a hole that is too big **or** too small will be unusable.)

In summary, the following define capability terminology. The use of clear and precise terms is the key to perfect communication, which will lead us to a successful operation.

Target	Perfect!
Tolerances	The amount of incompetence the customer will tolerate today.
Specification Limit	The calculated limits where the part, product, service, or process no longer meets the minimum functional requirement today. Totally unacceptable!

When we are calculating the strategic assessments, we use the following test based on whether we are testing on both sides or on one side only.

Specification	Criteria	Strategic Assessment
Upper Specification Limit or Service Level Agreement (SLAs)	Product above the upper specification limit	Greater than (upper specification limit)
Lower Specification Limit	Product below the lower specification limit	Less than (lower specification limit)
Specification Limit	Product outside the specification limits	Two tails (outside the specification limits)

A clear understanding of our capability terms of target, tolerance, and specification limits is crucial to an accurate capability study and effective strategic decisions. When we are analyzing a product, we must have a clear, objective way of assessing when the product or process is totally unacceptable. We must compare what we make to what the customer wants and will live with.

121

Now we can superimpose what we make onto where the customer's patience has been exceeded. This diagram, a capability study, now paints the picture of how we are doing in terms of our customers by adding the specification limits or SLAs to the chart.

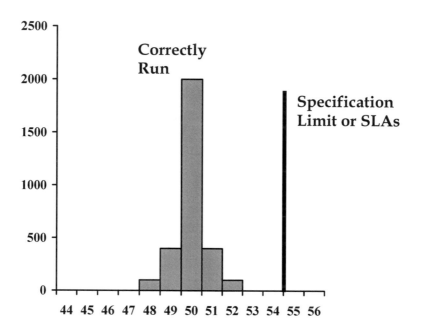

When we are analyzing a product or process, we now have a clear, objective way of assessing when the product or process is totally unacceptable, by comparing what we make to what the customer wants and will live with. This capability chart is the tool to provide the strategist with the call center's picture.

The typical capability discussion revolves around assessing whether the product will meet the customer's expectations. Focusing all of our attention on the product is a recipe for no improvement. Complete capability studies call for all process metrics to be assessed, as well as all product metrics. Always do capability studies on all product and process metrics for a complete assessment.

The strategic terms that we have covered are target, tolerance, specification limit, Service Level Agreements (SLA), product, process, and capability.

Strategic View

The Second Principle states that *Division of Labor, is the framework for all aspects of decision-making. It must be clearly understood to separate the policy, strategic, and tactical decisions. Operations makes the tactical decisions of running the facility. Management makes the strategic decisions of assessing the facility's suitability for the job. Executives make the policy decisions of providing the vision for the business.* Our focus for strategic reports must be focused around the strategic decisions of assessing the facility's suitability for the job. Before we cover the strategic view let's have a metric recap.

For proper numerical analysis technique, we must monitor both central tendency and variability.

0.0497	0.0508	0.0506	0.0502
0.0503	0.0509	0.0495	0.0505
0.0490	0.0496	0.0487	0.0497
0.0503	0.0492	0.0497	0.0499
0.0496	0.0510	0.0494	0.0495

The numbers above are call center phone pick up time measurements. The central tendency monitor of **average** is .0499. It is the balance point of the values and is shown in the chart below.

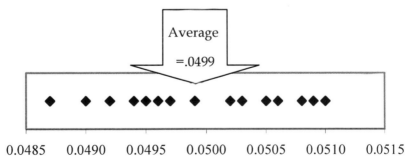

Variability is monitored by range and standard deviation. The chart below shows the range for the phone pick up time measurements.

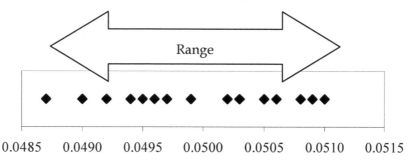

Failure to monitor these will lead to catastrophic mistakes. Now we will expand our discussion into a new area to cover how the data points are spread.

Where the Spread is Located

In the chapter on metric monitoring we used an example of three motel chains. The average cost was $25 per night for each chain. Motels B and C both had averages and standard deviations that are relatively similar. A new technique is required to show the difference for examples like this. The problem is that the magnitude of the central tendency and variability are similar.

Motel Location	A	B	C
Average	$25	$25	$25
Maximum	$27	$56	$40
Minimum	$23	$2	$10
Range	$4	$54	$30
Standard Deviation	$1	$9	$10

This new technique needs to show a different dimension. This dimension needs to represent, not the magnitude of the spread, but the location of the spread.

The first example (the person to the left) is a person whose shape is that of a body builder. His largest mass is located at the top of his body. The second example is someone who weighs the same as the first person. The difference between these two people is that the second person's mass is located in the center of his body. The third person is a person weighing about the same as the first two individuals. This person's mass is located at the bottom of his body.

All three drawings are similar but all three are different. The technique to differentiate between the three people needs to show the location of their spread. The drawings above do an excellent job of presenting this information. Let's discuss how we can prepare a picture of data that will present the location of the spread just like the pictures above show the people's location of their spread. This analysis is called data distribution.

125

Distribution

We will analyze a new set of data that we want to convert into a data distribution. We'll begin with a data set of call center pick up times measured in seconds.

Call #	Pick up Time	Call #	Pick up Time
1	57	21	51
2	62	22	48
3	58	23	56
4	58	24	56
5	59	25	54
6	58	26	43
7	62	27	52
8	55	28	57
9	68	29	56
10	51	30	51
11	50	31	55
12	65	32	51
13	50	33	61
14	49	34	63
15	66	35	44
16	52	36	55
17	57	37	56
18	47	38	61
19	55	39	53
20	50	40	70
Average Pick up Time			55.6
Standard Deviation			6.1

The particular aspect we will analyze is the pick up time. We have already calculated the average pick up time to be 55.6 seconds. The standard deviation is 6.1 seconds. In other words, the balance point of the pick up time is 55 seconds with the amount of spread being 6 seconds. Let's now begin to analyze the location of the spread or distribution of the calls' ages. To keep the following examples simple we will use a rounded average of 55 and a rounded standard deviation of 6. Not only do we need to know the center point and the magnitude of the spread, we also need to know where the spread is occurring.

The distribution answers the question, "Where Is The Spread?" From what we saw of the spread of the people's weights, the best way to analyze the distribution is through pictures. This is accomplished through either a frequency table or a histogram. The frequency table is the tabular means for analyzing where the data is distributed. The histogram is the pictorial technique for analyzing the distribution.

Frequency Table

Pick up Time Groups	Number of Calls
35-40	0
40⁺-45	2
45⁺-50	6
50⁺-55	12
55⁺-60	11
60⁺-65	6
65⁺-70	3
70⁺-75	0

A frequency table counts the items in the data that fall into a series of intervals. The example shown is the call center pick up times.

The pick up time group from 35 seconds to 40 seconds has no calls, +40 seconds to 45 seconds has two calls, and +45 seconds to 50 seconds has six calls. This chart continues for all of the pick up time groups.

Histogram

The histogram displays in pictorial form the measurement distribution and explains where the spread or concentration of values is occurring. The horizontal axis, or X-axis, shows how the measurement groups were formed in five-second increments. The vertical axis, or Y-axis, depicts the number of occurrences for each group.

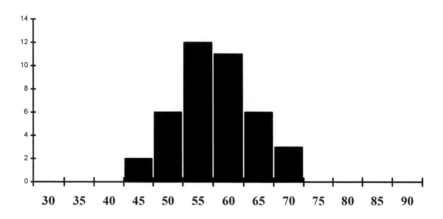

This chart is used to assess how well the distribution is fitted to a normal curve. The location of the spread of the pick up time is shown in the histogram above. From our prior statistics, we know the average pick up time of a call is 55 seconds. The bars that form the histogram are the tallest closest to this average. As the calls become longer (farther from the average), the number of occurrences drops rapidly above the average. As the calls become shorter, the number of occurrences drops at the same rate below the average. The bars above the average and below the average are symmetric to each other.

Normal Distribution

The bell curve is another name for the normal distribution, sometimes referred to as the Gaussian distribution. Normal distribution is described with the average as the central point of the measurements and the standard deviation as the variability of the measurements. The normal distribution is symmetric around its average. Fifty percent of the data points are above the average and fifty percent of the measurements are below the average. The frequency of occurrence (or the number of occurrences) drops rapidly as we move farther from the center. This characteristic is true both above and below the average. The frequencies of occurrences above and below the average are symmetric.

This chart depicts a picture of how the grade scores will look when the grades are published. The chart shows the spread of grades from an English literature class of thirty students. When the score measurements are converted to grades and look like the diagram, the process is well represented by a normal distribution. The perfect normal does not have the steps of a histogram but is a smooth curve.

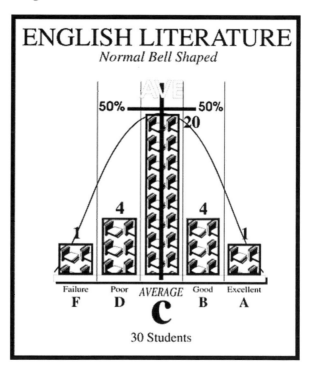

This chart shows how a typical class in English literature could have been graded using a bell-shaped curve. Out of a class of thirty students twenty would receive a "C", four would receive a "B", another four would receive a "D", one would receive an "A", and one would receive an "F".

We will do another example for our analysis.

The following is a school district IT help desk. The IT help desk call volume by day is shown in the table below. We have already computed the average, range, and standard deviation. Now we will build a frequency table, construct a histogram, and check for normality.

Call Center Call Volume								
Date	Day of Week	# of Calls	Date	Day of Week	# of Calls	Date	Day of Week	# of Calls
5/22	Mon	40	6/27	Tue	34	8/7	Mon	36
5/23	Tue	44	6/28	Wed	34	8/8	Tue	37
5/24	Wed	46	6/29	Thr	36	8/9	Wed	37
5/25	Thr	39	6/30	Fri	36	8/10	Thr	34
5/26	Fri	45	7/6	Thr	35	8/11	Fri	35
6/5	Mon	34	7/7	Fri	37	8/14	Mon	39
6/6	Tue	37	7/10	Mon	36	8/15	Tue	43
6/7	Wed	39	7/11	Tue	33	8/16	Wed	40
6/8	Thr	39	7/12	Wed	34	8/17	Thr	43
6/9	Fri	34	7/13	Thr	38	8/18	Fri	44
6/12	Mon	36	7/14	Fri	36	8/21	Mon	46
6/13	Tue	35	7/17	Mon	38	8/22	Tue	44
6/14	Wed	35	7/18	Tue	35	8/23	Wed	45
6/15	Thr	34	7/19	Wed	36	8/24	Thr	43
6/16	Fri	37	7/20	Thr	32	8/25	Fri	39
6/19	Mon	34	7/21	Fri	33	8/28	Mon	47
6/20	Tue	37	7/24	Mon	39	8/29	Tue	43
6/21	Wed	32	7/25	Tue	32	8/30	Wed	43
6/22	Thr	39	7/26	Wed	38	8/31	Thr	44
6/23	Fri	35	7/27	Thr	38	9/1	Fri	42
6/26	Mon	36	7/28	Fri	34	9/5	Tue	44

The help desk call volume average is 38.1 calls and has a standard deviation is 4.1 calls.

Now we will prepare and analyze the call volume histogram.

The call volume has two peaks in the distribution. One group is formed at the 35 and 37 bars. A second peak is formed at the 45 bar.

The data distribution for this example shows a non-normal distribution.

	# of Calls
Average	38.1
Standard Deviation	4.1

Time Groups	Count
0-31	0
31⁺-33	5
33⁺-35	15
35⁺-37	14
37⁺-39	11
39⁺-41	2
41⁺-43	6
43⁺-45	7
45⁺-47	3

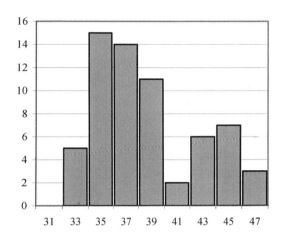

Why Is the Normal Distribution Important?

There are three reasons why the normal distribution is important.

The first reason is data that is well represented by a normal distribution allows us to predict using the probabilities of the normal. Your metric analyst should have a really good understanding of how to compute these predictions. For the purposes of this book a conceptual under standing of these probabilities is important, and we will look at them in more detail in a few pages.

The second reason is that non-normal distributions like the one above may be improperly grouped. This reason has become a common problem as our centers have evolved from the single-use call center to the five call center types.

The third reason is that non-normal distributions are probably an indication that the call center is not being run correctly and consistently.

In summary, here are the three reasons the normal distribution is important

- Projection for assessing the centers
- Checking for proper groups
- Assess whether the center is running correctly and consistently

Resolving these issues allows us to reduce wait time, provide better service, and reduce cost. We will cover the details in the next chapter.

From the analysis of the original call pick up times we can conclude that the call times are normally distributed. Thus we can use the probabilities of the normal to make predictions. Now we need to learn the normal probabilities so that we can use them for predictions.

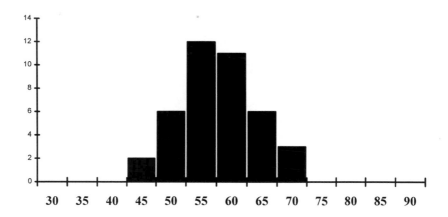

Predicting Call Center Results

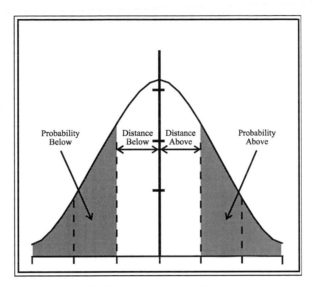

All measurements that track like a normal distribution have a very definite set of probabilities. Since the normal distribution is symmetric, the probabilities above and below the average are exactly the same.

This chart shows the symmetry when the distance above and below the average is equal. When the distances are equal, the area under the normal curve is the same above and below the average. Since the bell is symmetrical, we can focus our attention on the "distance above" side, because the same calculations and probability will apply for the "distance below" side.

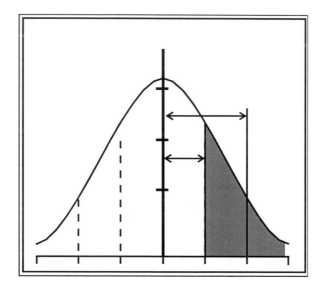

As the distance away from the mean, or center, of a normal distribution gets bigger, the probability gets smaller.

The area under the curve represents the probability of occurrence. An occurrence outside plus or minus one standard deviation from the average equates to a probability of 16% above or 16% below or 68% inside. A point outside plus or minus two standard deviation equates to a probability of 2.3% above or 2.3% below or 95.4% inside. Then outside plus or minus three standard deviation equates to a probability of .1% above or .1% below or 99.8% inside.

NORMAL
DISTRIBUTION

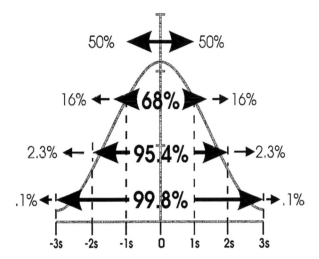

With these probabilities, we can make predictions about our call center and how well we are meeting the SLA.

Returning to the English literature class, how were the different letter grades determined? First the "C" grades were inside the range of plus or minus one standard deviation. In this range, the probability is 68%. Thus, the 20 students receiving a C grade are 68% of the total 30.

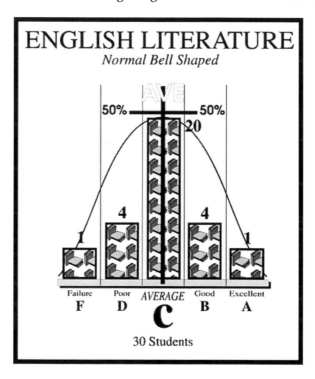

Notice that 95.4% of the grades fall in the plus or minus two standard deviations. Of these, 68% have already received their C grade leaving a total of 27% receiving a B or a D. Since the normal distribution is symmetric, half of the students and those above the average will receive a B--that is 13% or four B grades. The remaining four students in the low end of this range will receive a D grade. Now 99.8% of the grades fall in plus or minus three standard deviations. Similarly, 95.4% have already received a B, C, or D. The remaining 4.4%, or two students, will receive an F or A grade. The student on the low side of the average will receive the F while the student on the high side of the average will receive the A.

Expanding the prediction area we can build a table that will show spots where our call center metrics will fall.

The distance away from the average as a function of the metric standard deviation	Probability outside the point	Percent of the call center outside a point
1	16%	16 out of 100
2	2.3%	2.3 out of 100
3	.1%	1 out of 1,000
4	.003%	3 out of 100,000
5	.00003%	3 out of 10 million
6	.0000001%	2 out of 1 billion

Now we can use these predictions in our call center and support the strategic role of assessing the center capability.

In our chapter on strategic terms we discussed the need for SLAs. These SLAs must be developed for predicting an individual call and its results.

Since call center complexity has radically increased, the SLAs must continually be assessed for their accuracy and validity. The days of being able to use a simple average for an SLA passed away in the evolution to five different call center types. In our multifunction centers, variability and distribution are of equal importance to central tendency. To monitor variability and the data distribution, we must have the individual call information to analyze.

With good, well-formed SLAs we can now compare what our customer will tolerate to what our center is actually doing. First, we can superimpose the two issues on one histogram. The SLA shows the spot we would declare our service to be totally unacceptable to any one of our customers.

The chart below is an example of this combination. This chart gives us an excellent strategic view.

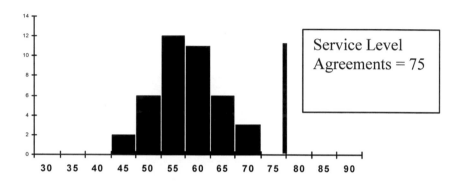

The metric analyst or your metric computer system prepares the strategic view by superimposing the actual metric measurements onto the SLA and calculating the predictions. The chart is a strategic view called a capability study. The bar reflects the actual measurements showing the number of occurrences by group. The line is the SLA.

Now let's prepare a complete strategic view of a metric.

We will analyze a call center that processes customer orders from a mailed brochure. Since this call center is the company storefront and a source of our company's revenue, our agents must answer calls in a timely manner. The profile of our typical caller is at about 20 seconds our customers will drop off the line and we lose the opportunity to make the sale. Our call center strategic decision-makers decide that all calls must be answered within 20 seconds, which provides our pick up time SLA for our call center.

The following are the times, in seconds, till pick up of five consecutive calls received on the hour. First we'll plot the control charts. Then, we will develop a complete capability study validating all assumptions.

	1:00	2:00	3:00	4:00	5:00	6:00	7:00	8:00	9:00	10:00
1	14.08	14.05	11.25	17.24	18.19	17.19	18.77	19.34	17.41	15.59
2	12.36	21.02	14.56	16.17	16.15	15.96	11.81	19.44	11.41	17.06
3	12.27	20.95	16.42	16.75	12.25	15.14	12.78	13.37	14.75	14.81
4	16.06	19.23	13.41	15.87	14.89	17.18	15.06	11.75	13.96	14.65
5	15.61	15.28	16.50	13.81	19.31	17.21	16.97	18.06	14.85	16.31

	11:00	12:00	13:00	14:00	15:00	16:00	17:00	18:00	19:00	20:00
1	16.74	14.33	16.57	14.50	12.40	16.11	10.56	13.59	9.44	19.63
2	12.36	14.84	15.47	17.51	8.96	12.29	15.05	14.07	13.80	16.99
3	10.64	14.72	14.73	13.75	18.77	14.88	16.26	11.80	17.34	14.57
4	8.79	10.72	16.97	11.34	19.63	14.02	14.37	18.10	15.81	19.65
5	14.62	12.87	14.94	18.73	19.06	13.17	11.50	15.11	13.73	18.32

	21:00	22:00	23:00	24:00	1:00	2:00	3:00	4:00	5:00	6:00
1	14.39	13.21	10.58	19.84	11.44	15.95	14.40	14.93	11.99	19.23
2	12.60	13.03	12.66	15.05	16.35	11.78	13.29	11.58	15.11	13.99
3	16.75	16.86	16.47	9.91	16.48	16.35	10.69	12.65	10.02	15.31
4	17.48	13.08	15.38	14.78	18.90	13.51	13.49	12.51	18.97	13.79
5	16.82	16.90	11.84	14.10	14.41	11.28	16.65	14.62	17.45	14.50

First we must test the tactical issues. The call center's time-until-pick up data is posted onto X-bar and R control charts. These X-bar charts below monitor central tendency. These R charts below monitor variability.

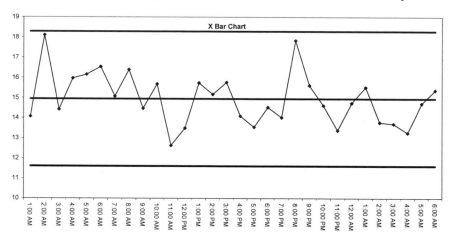

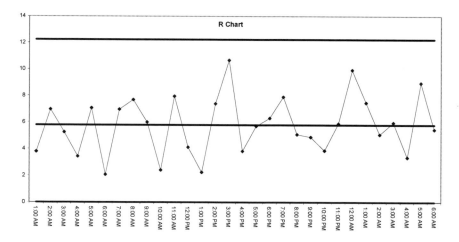

The X-bar and R control charts show that the process is in control. This means the tactical workforce has done their role of correctly and consistently running this call center. With this knowledge in hand, the capability study may continue.

The histogram of time-until-pick up data of individual calls is shown below. This histogram shows a well-formed bell curve. This allows the use of a normal table to project the call pick up time that will fall above the SLA of 20 seconds.

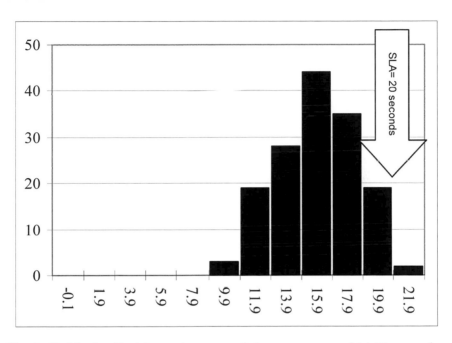

The individual call pick up times result in an average of 14.95 seconds with a standard deviation of 2.62 seconds. Our call center metric analyst builds the table below. We projects that 2.68% of the calls will exceed the SLA of 20 seconds. These projections are based on the results of the actual individual calls and the predictions based on the normal distribution computed by our metric analyst or metric software.

	Strategic View of Pick up Time
	Percent Above the SLA of 20 Seconds
Predicted	2.682%
Actual	2 of 150 or 1.33%

Our predicted percent above the SLA is 2.68% and we have actually experienced about 1.33% above the SLA. This percentage is high because

141

of our lost revenue. We should investigate ways to change the facility so that the time to pick up is reduced.

We will continue to the next chapter to cover how the strategic decision-makers can use this strategic view to improve our call center.

Chapter Nine:
Using the Strategic View

Division of Labor drives the decision-making process. It dictates who will be in charge of the different kinds of decisions (strategic or tactical). We are doomed if the managers fail to fully grasp Division of Labor. The following table shows a summary of Division of Labor and the three decision types.

	Executive	Management	Operations
Decisions	Policy	Strategic	Tactical
Terms	Vision	Capability	Control
Tools for Decisions	Market research, Financial reports	Strategic Views from Capability Studies, Service Level Agreements	Tactical View from Control Chart, Control Limits, Targets
Duties	Provide and share the vision	Build a Plan and assess the impact of change	Execute the plan and detect change
Functions	Develop a business vision	Provide the Resources, Time, & Place to resolve plan changes	Detect change, Determine cause

From our discussion of Division of Labor we know that executives make policy decisions. Policy decisions require information, which involves the classic financial reports. Below is an example of a policy report of the revenue of the business.

Revenue											
2001											
Jan	Feb	Mar	Apr	May	Jun	Jul	Aug	Sep	Oct	Nov	Dec
$ 404,469	$ 446,624	$ 347,164	$ 329,862	$ 386,716	$ 351,994	$ 373,752	$ 432,657	$ 354,479	$ 324,049	$ 395,372	$ 396,130

These reports are done monthly to show the business progress. These reports have month over month layout to put the current month into context. These reporting methods work well to support that mission and clearly support the policy decision-making. All reports and metrics must have a clear objective that they support. These policy reports do meet their objective.

Imagine that the center we are running is an order-processing center. The business spends money on direct mail brochures to convince the customers to buy their products. The call center is the storefront for our business, the place where all revenue comes in.

Since executives are used to seeing these policy reports, they assume that the same format will work for strategic call center reports. We prepare reports that look like the ones below using the policy format. We monitor the abandonment rate, or dropped calls, for our center. We are also monitoring the percent of calls that fall below the SLA of 20-second pickup time.

	Phone Metrics											
	2001											
	Jan	Feb	Mar	Apr	May	Jun	Jul	Aug	Sep	Oct	Nov	Dec
Abandonment	1.5%	0.7%	1.7%	0.6%	0.7%	0.8%	0.9%	1.1%	1.4%	0.7%	1.6%	1.8%
Answer within 20 sec	88%	95%	84%	96%	94%	93%	88%	89%	89%	92%	89%	86%

We add some graphics to the report and begin to feel that our reporting is good. The call center is the revenue base, and each customer is a value. Because of our direct mail cost and the potential revenue each call brings to the company, a single dropped call is too many.

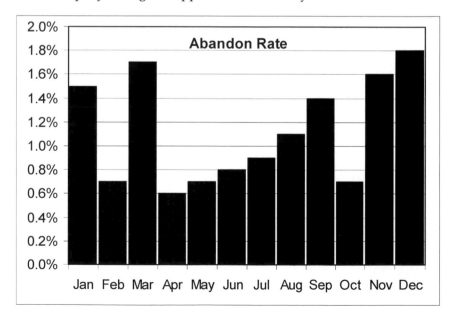

Let's look in more detail to see what happened in the last month on the graph, the month of December. The chart below is a daily look at the abandonment rate. This chart displays the percent of people that got so frustrated that they hung up before we could take their order. The monthly report shows a bad sign but when we look at each day we see several spikes that are much worse. These peaks and valleys could not be seen in the monthly look.

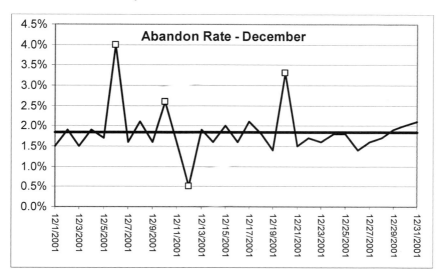

Our strategic decisions are to provide the facility and to assist in the running of the center. Our strategic call center decision-maker cannot use this monthly report to support those missions because the information is not timely. We need to assess and change the call center facility in an almost real-time manner. Even looking at the daily report we have no information as to what to do. The reports are well intended, but the road to hell is paved with good intentions.

We need timely information that answers many questions. How will we know how to stop the dropped calls? How will we know what the cause of the dropped calls is? In Chapter Two we covered the metric format and metric blueprint. These will allow our strategic decision-maker to take a proactive approach to running the center.

Chapter Nine

Operational Philosophy

Call centers reside in a rapid, changing, and dynamic world. The environment requires timely, focused, and appropriate information. The change management philosophy allows us to use the tactician to detect change so that once we have a strategic baseline we only have to reassess the center when a change occurs in the center. These changes must be assessed immediately, so that each change can be managed.

We cannot manage a metric like abandonment--we can only react to it. We must understand the drivers and then manage those drivers. These metric drivers must then have a decision support structure for proactive decisions.

Metrics and Science

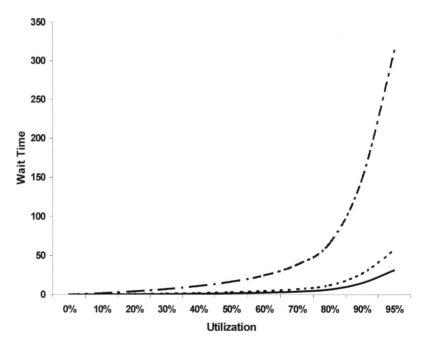

Grocery store designers and managers built new and better techniques based on metrics and science. Call center strategic decision-makers must also use metrics, a metric blueprint, and science to build and manage state of the art call centers. As an example, our proactive strategic decision-maker understands that we must manage processing time central tendency, processing time variability, and agent utilization to manage wait time and abandonment.

Strategists and Tacticians

Our strategist must trust that the tactical supervisors and agents are doing their role. Running the call center is clearly tactical and the job of the tactical decision-maker. These tactical decisions are noting when a change in the process and product metrics has occurred, alerting management when a change has occurred so that the strategic decision-maker can assess the impact of the change on the product or the process, finding the cause of a change, working with the strategic decision maker in deciding what action to take, having the process knowledge to know when and what adjustments are required.

Peak efficiency is dependent on strategists providing a correct and capable facility, which includes both physical and intellectual assets. The tactical work force must count on the strategic players to do their end of the bargain.

Providing the call center facility is clearly strategic and the job of the strategic decision-maker. These strategic decisions are

- Providing the tools, methods, structure, and technology to meet the policy vision of the executive.
- Assessing the impact on the customer or user when a change in the process and product metrics has occurred.
- Dynamically retooling the center to meet business changes.

Since strategy and tactics are very different, a different metric view for each seems logical. The tactical view supports the need to detect a change. The strategic metric view supports the assessment of how well the center is performing, as a function of the customer's needs.

Our strategic reports will look at each of the following:

- Grouping
- Metric Description
  - Central Tendency
  - Variability
  - Distribution
- Predictions

147

Failure to monitor all three characteristics as a team will lead to catastrophic mistakes. Grouping, metric description, and predictions form an essential team that allows us to vividly understand, monitor, and make informed decisions about our call centers.

We have already covered metric description and predictions, which we will use to understand grouping issues.

Metric Grouping

There are three grouping types: 1) Physical, 2) Associational, and 3) Time-series. **Physical groups** are those groups that are physically of like kind. **Associational Groups** are physically the same but form groups because the analytical numbers are different. **Time-series groups** are from groups over time.

Homogeneous groups may seem obvious to one person and not to another. Thus clear guidelines are required. Control is another way of saying homogeneous or consistent. We must never allow a mixture of non-homogeneous groups. We cannot mix size 12 and size 9 shoes together in a homogeneous group. Neither can we mix blue shirts with white shirts. An average of a size 10½ shoe or a pale blue shirt would be misleading. Instead, simple common sense is required to properly prepare homogeneous groups. It appears to be obvious to keep groups separate, but this is not always the case. Grouping requirements may be difficult to conceptualize and even harder to assure.

Time-series Groups

The following is the school district IT help desk call volume analysis that we covered in the last chapter. We are using this simple example because most of us have or know of someone who has children in school. As we do this example remember that school is out during the

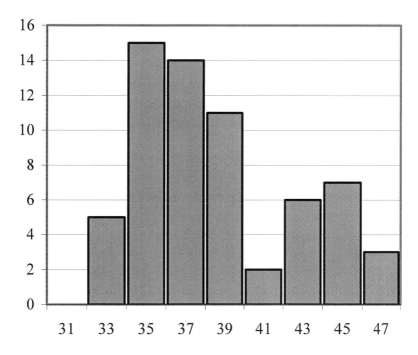

summer months. The call volume metric average is 38.1 calls and the variability monitored by standard deviation is 4.1 calls. The following graph describes our metric distribution. The distribution was non-normal.

The call volume has two peaks in the distribution. One group is formed at the 35 and 37 bars. A second peak is formed at the 45 bar. The school district IT help desk call volume distribution is not a normal distribution. Rather than just stop, grouping analysis should be done. The easiest way to check for a time-series group problem is to plot the data in time-series sequence. The chart below is a plot of our call center's daily call volume in chronological sequence.

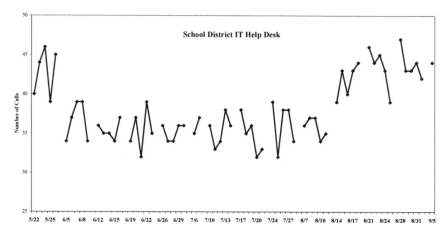

Looking at the time series graph, two distinct groups are seen. Group one represents a lower call volume than group two. This school district ends its school session on May 27 and resumes for the next school year on August 14. Without this information the time-series plot still shows the two distinct call volume groups. With the date information we can now see that the call volume changes to a lower level when school is out. The date information allows you to determine the reason for the time difference. With two groups identified, separate studies should be done.

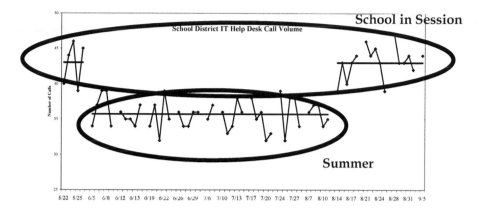

Let's split the call volume into two groups and recalculate our metric description.

First, the school summer vacation call volume is studied. The results show a lower average than when school was in session. This makes sense because no teachers and students are in the school, only administrative personnel. The summer average is 35.6 calls with a standard deviation of 2.0 calls. The distribution is normal.

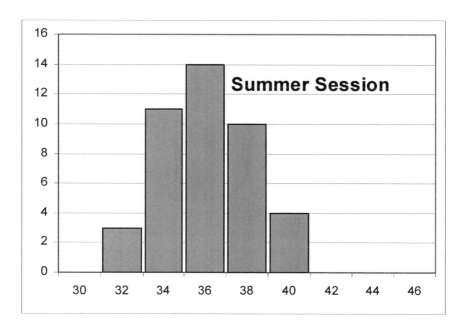

Second, a study is done using the data when school is in session. The results show larger call volumes because of the added traffic of the teachers and students. The school in session average is 43.0 calls with a standard deviation of 2.4 calls. The distribution is also normal.

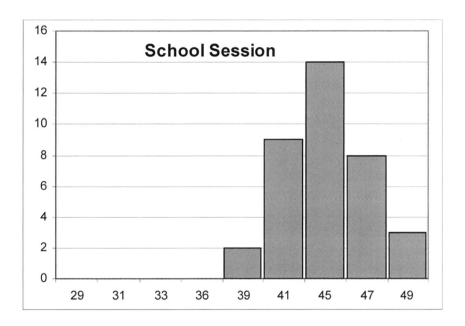

This is a simple example but notice by properly grouping the metric we can cut the variability in half. The lumped call volume metric average is 38.1 calls and the variability monitored by standard deviation is 4.1 calls. The summer average is 35.6 calls with a standard deviation of 2.0 calls. The school in session average is 43.0 calls with a standard deviation of 2.4 calls.

Call Volume			
	Average	Standard Deviation	Distribution
Overall or Lumped	38.1	4.1	Non-normal or bimodal
Summer	35.6	2.0	Normal
School in Session	43.0	2.4	Normal

When the average for each group is superimposed onto the time-phased graph, a clear time-series group pattern is seen. Using the tactical view allows us to test and assure these time-series groups. Our strategist will want to see and analyze both the tactical and strategic views.

The following shows the tactical view of the school help desk call volume.

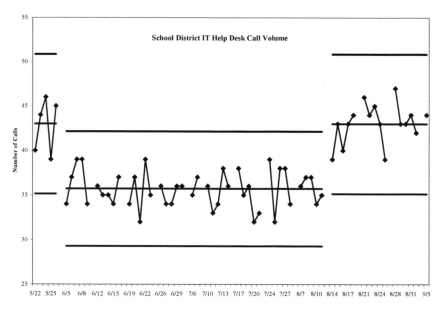

If we had not tested the time-series groups and identified the two distinct groups, our expectations and decisions would have been very wrong. Using all the values with no grouping separation, our expected year-round call volume would have been an overall average of 38 calls and a standard deviation of four calls. The strategist would have established a facility (staff, number of phone lines, etc.) to support these levels. When school was in session, the center based on the metric view would be too small. During the summer, the center based on that faulty metric view would be too large. During the summer the center staffing would have too many people and during the school session we would not have enough agents to handle the call volume.

This only takes into account the faulty average. The standard deviation with all the days included is four calls. If we had grouped properly the standard deviation during summer would be two calls and the in session standard deviation would be 2.4 calls. In the queuing discussion and the grocery store example remember what a huge driver variability was in our wait time. A doubled variability will have a tremendous impact on every aspect of the call center facility. Establishing proper groups so that variability is small will allow us to radically improve everything about the call center. Like the grocery store example we can and will build express lanes in our call center.

From this simple example we can see the importance of grouping. In your center some examples that may require analysis are seasonality, core hours versus off peak hours, weekends versus weekdays, the start of week versus the rest of the week, cycles, etc.

With time series groups covered we will now move to associational groups and then on to physical groups.

Associational Group

Associational groups are things of like analytical kind. These are the hardest to conceptualize. Machines that are similar, one machine running at ten percent defect versus another machine running at zero percent defect, are physically the same but associationally different.

Agents processing calls may physically be the same but associationally different. An agent example could be airline reservations, hotel resort reservations, or IT help desks. Don't confuse associational grouping with skill-based routing where the tasks are different. These examples are for the same skill and process (think grocery store checkout regular and express lanes) but the metrics are different. Once a group is identified, the challenge is understanding why it has occurred.

Association is another way of saying that we only group those things of like kind. These groups are then called homogeneous. Non-homogeneous items must never be placed in the same group for analytical reports.

The following table shows the processing time of several types of calls into an IT help desk. The help desk's call support types are desktop, product support, billing, sales, and networking.

Desktop	Product Support	Billing	Sales	Network
17.55	20.19	26.40	35.70	101.00
17.60	20.20	26.65	36.05	125.00
18.00	20.25	26.70	36.20	156.00
18.00	20.45	26.70	37.25	182.00
18.35	20.50	26.78	37.25	182.00
18.45	20.65	27.00	37.35	137.00
18.50	20.70	27.11	38.30	199.00
18.75	20.85	27.20	38.40	207.00
19.15	21.10	27.20	39.00	132.00
19.25	21.10	27.25	39.40	147.00
19.65	21.20	27.35	39.55	176.00
19.65	21.25	27.45	40.54	157.00
19.68	21.25	27.90	40.80	114.00
19.70	21.30	27.95	43.60	98.00

If all the calls are lumped together with no grouping, the average and standard deviation of call volume would be 51.22 and 52.94 respectively. Should these values be used in a study?

The five call types have their grouped results calculated below.

	All Type	Desk-top	Product Support	Billing	Sales	Net-work
Average	51.22	18.73	20.79	27.12	38.53	150.93
Std Deviation	52.94	.78	.42	.46	2.17	35.05
N	70	14	14	14	14	14

Each product type's call processing time is plotted on the graph below. For some groups, the individual call processing time is so similar that the plot points almost take the form of one large point while the networking area is very diverse and each network processing time

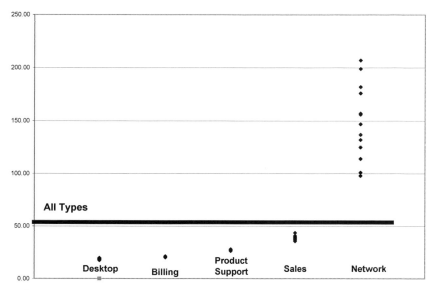

varies.

Grouping the calls together while ignoring the analytical differences makes the average worthless. This can be seen visually on the scatter plot above. The average for all types is shown as a straight line horizontally across the graph. The all-type average is not close to any value and is useless. Also, the all-type standard deviation (52.94) is radically larger than any of the individual groups' standard deviation (desktop .78, product support .42, billing .46, sales 2.17, and network 35.05). Using the all-type standard deviation would create the erroneous impression of much higher variability than is truly the case. Separate studies should be done for each group.

For a second associational grouping example, the table below shows the call center pickup times for six call centers. Analyze the pickup times to see which of the six centers' results can be grouped together.

Call Pickup Time in minutes					
Center 1	Center 2	Center 3	Center 4	Center 5	Center 6
0.32	0.32	0.66	0.44	0.22	0.73
0.31	0.50	0.67	0.55	0.08	0.42
0.49	0.25	0.26	0.51	0.39	0.42
0.67	0.40	0.69	0.75	0.13	0.52
0.57	0.30	0.41	0.34	0.23	0.33
0.62	0.18	0.36	0.57	0.38	0.41
0.49	0.20	0.44	0.49	0.34	0.49
0.48	0.28	0.43	1.03	0.27	0.52
0.52	0.55	0.63	0.52	0.17	0.48
0.63	0.08	0.76	0.51	0.65	0.57
Average 0.51	0.31	0.53	0.57	0.29	0.49
Standard Deviation 0.12	0.14	0.17	0.19	0.16	0.11

Confidence intervals are the tools your metrics analyst will use to determine which centers should be grouped. The confidence intervals are now plotted on the graph below. We can see that centers 1, 3, 4, and 6 form a high pickup time rate group, and centers 2 and 5 form a low pickup time rate group.

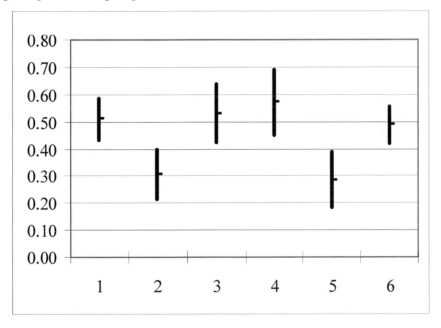

Physical Groups

Members of physical groups are things having like kind such as type, size, or color. For proper analysis, physically different items should not be mixed into one group. The following compares call volume in the Atlanta center to the Dallas center. The Atlanta center is a workmen's compensation claims processing center while the Dallas center is a life insurance claims processing center. Each center processes very different information. This example is to test if there is a difference in the call volume average between the centers.

	Call Volume
	213
	174
	172
	173
	187
Atlanta workmen's compensation claims center	230
	167
	163
	196
	196
	199
	161
	194
	214

	Call Volume
	152
	211
	191
	122
	125
Dallas life insurance claims center	118
	192
	143
	131
	94
	112
	203

This example is designed to show physically differing groups. This example tests whether there is a difference in the call volume between the Atlanta and Dallas call centers. The Atlanta call center's average is 189 with a standard deviation of 21. The Dallas call center's average is 150 with a standard deviation of 40.

Your metric analyst can build a graph of the mean plot, which clarifies where the data form groups. The mean plot is one of the tools for discrete group comparisons. The confidence intervals do not overlap, indicating that the Dallas center should form one group, while the Atlanta center should form a second group. The Atlanta center has more volume than the Dallas center.

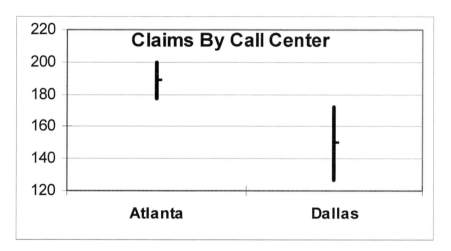

Call Center Grouping Examples

Time-series Groups

The following are some examples of time-series groups that you might want to look for in your center. These situations could include an analysis of seasonality like the Christmas season. We could have time-series groups between our core hours versus off peak hours. Weekends compared to weekdays might be another time-series example in a call center. Many times you will see a spike at the start of the week versus the rest of the week. One other example is some kind of a cycle with a recurring theme.

Associational Groups

Our business's financial exposure sometimes will cause the need for associational groups. This grouping need might exist in large insurance claims that are out of the norm. Revenue, many times, creates the need for an associational group where we give special treatment to those who spend the most. Businesses and products may need to have associational groups formed. Another example is emergency calls that need grouping.

Physical Groups

The geography or location of our center or user may necessitate a grouping analysis. Different processes will need to be separated and grouped. The technology (like POT and VOIP) that we use may need a grouping methodology. The technology groups become more and more important as we move to new and different technologies. We will want to develop groups for vendors and clients. Another group would be formed for call status like criticality and priority.

In summary, our groups must form one (homogeneous) universe based on physical similarity, associational characteristics, and time-series groups. We can change the scenario, but correct formation of a group is critical to any report or analysis. The product and process data must be kept separate by grouping so that we can identify homogeneous groups and be able to form an aggregate group. An aggregate group is composed of things of like kind. With properly formed groups we can expect proper information leading to better decision-making

All our analyses are based on the assurance that both proper technique and proper grouping have been used. This combination allows us to provide good information. This analysis requires a bottom-up strategy of data collection and analysis.

Our data collection objective is to provide information to support better decision-making. Each piece of data should have the clear purpose of supporting a specific decision, and this purpose should be clearly stated for all who are gathering the data. By having a clear purpose as the environment changes, the data gatherers can adjust the manner in which they collect the data. Should the specific decision no longer be needed, then the data collection can also be discontinued.

Management needs information to make intelligent decisions. This information must be prepared in a format that concisely and accurately presents factual data. The problem with a detailed analysis is that one can become overwhelmed with data. We can "lose the forest for the trees" if we don't condense. The trick is to condense without making grouping mistakes. This grouping is to aggregate the data (summarize the data of like kind) to carefully and logically create a series of homogeneous groups for summary.

For us to do the detailed analysis that will lead to accurate reporting, a great deal of data gathering will be required and this is exactly what computers were meant to do. To adequately handle the detailed reporting, each call must have its data retained for our analysis. To support proper group formation, a bottom-up strategy of data reporting is required. This bottom-up group or individual call formation will test for groups. Proper grouping will allow correct and accurate information to flow to top management. With better information in hand, better decision-making can be expected.

Now we have completed all aspects of strategic reports. Our strategic reports will include the following: 1) Grouping, 2) Metric Description (central tendency, variability, and distribution), and 3) Predictions.

Strategic Decisions

These strategic decisions are

- Provide the tools, methods, structure, and technology to meet the policy vision of the executive.
- Assess the impact on the customer or user when a change in the process and product metrics has occurred.
- Dynamically retool the center to meet business changes.

The strategic metric view supports the assessment of how well the center is performing, as a function of the customer's needs. The three components that describe our metrics must be viewed as a team and assessed as a complete package. The strategist's decisions are directly impacted by proper metrics. Understanding the impact of each can yield profound improvement in our call center.

Chapter Summary

The strategic decision–makers must build metrics and the center with proper groups. There are three grouping types:

- Physical
- Associational
- Time-series

Physical groups are those groups that are physically of like kind. **Associational Groups** are physically the same but form groups because the analytical numbers are different. **Time-series groups** are from groups over time.

Providing your call center facility is clearly strategic and the job of the strategic decision-maker. These strategic decisions are

- Provide the tools, methods, structure, and technology to meet the policy vision of the executive.
- Assess the impact on the customer or user when a change in the process and product metrics has occurred.
- Dynamically retool the center to meet business changes.

Now the tactical and strategic decision-makers have formed a team each understanding their role and each decision-maker executing their role. Now we can have an effective center that is run, managed, and maintained.

Chapter Ten:
Strategic Decisions Using Metrics

Providing the Call Center Facility

We will now take a look at what's involved in providing the call center facility and how metrics will be used. We are really engineering the call center. Many times when we discuss the engineering associated with a call center, we focus only on the technology issues. Engineering the call center must apply to every asset from the technology to the people to the intellectual assets of how to run the facility. Our objective is to provide the tools, methods, structure, and technology to meet the policy vision of the executive.

Policy vision will vary from company to company and the policy may be different for different functions within the same company. The company's sales contact center may never want to tolerate a dropped call. This same company may allow longer waits for the customer service center where the customer calls to check the status of an order. Even longer waits might be acceptable in the warranty area. Each call center metric must have a well thought out policy on how we choose to treat our customers or users. These policies should regularly be reviewed to assure that they are still in line with any revisions or changes in the business climate.

Physical Assets

Physical assets like phones, lines, bandwidth, ACD, PBX, etc. must be engineered and sized to fit the needs of your policy.

Intellectual Assets

Intellectual assets are the processes, agents' knowledge, scripts, knowledge databases, number of agents, agent skill sets, etc. The center's intellectual assets must also be engineered and sized to meet the business policy.

Engineering the Center

Engineering the call center must be done for both physical and intellectual assets. Physical assets may require traffic science to engineer

165

the proper technology, proper number, and size, while intellectual assets may be engineered with queuing science. Both the physical and intellectual assets will require some assumptions of our metric descriptions of central tendency, variability, and distribution. Once we engineer the center, then we will use our tactical and strategic view to test our assumptions.

The first step is to develop the center process for the particular area that we engineered. As an example we are a software company that sells a point of sale software product in the retail trade. Our example is the company's IT help desk that supports desktop users, new user setup, finance questions, point of sale software support, and network issues.

Now we develop processes for each area in the center. For this book, we will just focus on the point of sale software support. Below is our first process dependency diagram with metric blueprint.

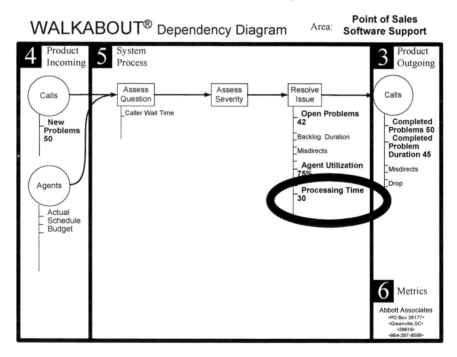

So that we have an example that we can see complete, we will focus on just call processing time circled on the metric blueprint. The same logic that we have prepared for this metric would also be used for every metric on the blueprint. For this metric we will need a script as to what the agent must say, what the agent does, and when to escalate a call.

The processing time that we have established has a target of 30 minutes from an analysis of the script. This target should match the average when we monitor the metric. Also the call center designer must estimate the variability that we would expect in this area.

We have also set an SLA for the call processing time metric to 45 minutes. As we establish our processing time, let's revisit our understanding of central tendency and variability.

Note the two distributions below both have an average of 30 minutes. The top graph has a large variation while the bottom graph has a small variation. With this knowledge we can improve the engineering design of our call center. All tactical and strategic decision-makers must appreciate the importance of variability on this metric, plus this metric's affect on other metrics.

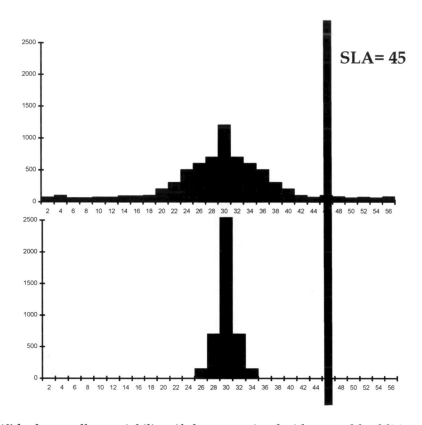

With the smaller variability, if the strategist decides to add additional information into the script, then we will not exceed the SLA. If the SLA is reduced (e.g. SLA = 40 minutes) the top scenario is in trouble, while the bottom scenario would still be very capable. This is just a few of the many strategic options that are available when we manage and keep our variability low. With the top graph of high variability, there are no options available to the strategist. This reinforces the need to communicate to our entire tactical workforce, both supervisors and agents, the importance of following the plan. This is similar to the express lane grocery store clerk not having people with more than ten items in their lane. Brilliant tactical execution is vital to the effective operation of a call center.

Our grocery store checkout example showed the impact of the driving factors on wait time. Just as in the grocery store, call center wait time is a function of utilization of the agent or rep, processing time average, and the processing time variability. In the grocery store and a call center, low waits don't just happen. We must design the center and then manage the center to obtain the desired results. The express lanes are a function of the driving factors and a scientific design.

Science and Strategic Metrics: Developing Express Lanes

This IT help desk supports desktop users, new user setup, finance questions, point of sale software support, and network issues. The five call center areas with their metric descriptions are listed below. The metric descriptions are estimates that we will track, monitor, and validate.

	Call Processing Time in Minutes					
	All Type	Desktop	New User Setup	Finance	Point of Sale - Product	Network
Average	51	19	21	27	30	150
Std Devia-tion	53	.8	.4	.5	3	35

Grouping the products together while ignoring the differences makes the average worthless. The all-type average is not close to any value and is useless. Also, the all-type standard deviation of 53 minutes is radically larger than any of the individual group's standard deviation. The individual area standard deviations are desktop .8 minutes, new user setup .4 minutes, financial support .4 minutes, point of sale product support 3 minutes, and network 35 minutes. Using the all-type standard deviation would create the erroneous impression of much higher variability than is truly the case.

The all types has an average of 51 minutes and a standard deviation of 53 minutes. The all-type average is not close to any value and is useless. If all the agents try to do every type of call we must use these to calculate our wait time and the waits will be unnecessarily high. To reduce these waits our strategist will have to radically reduce the agent utilization. The reduction in utilization can only be achieved by adding agents, which will increase our cost.

The all-type standard deviation is 53 minutes and is radically larger than any of the individual groups. Call center wait time is a function of utilization of the agent or rep, processing time average, and the processing time variability. With each individual area having lower variability, then we should keep the call types separate. The use of variability allows us to have lower wait times at higher utilizations. We are back to having it all. With each area forming an express lane, we will have lower wait time and lower cost because the smaller variability allows us to push the utilization higher. One other benefit is that since our agents work in a specific express lane area like point of sale support, all their calls will be about that topic. This specialization will give us better answers to our calls.

The order of magnitude of improvement by applying metrics and science is huge.

Assessing the Impact

With our IT help desk scientifically designed and built, we will monitor and manage each metric. We will assess the impact on the customer or user when a change in the process and product metrics has occurred. The following are our call processing time tactical charts that validate our design estimates of central tendency and variability.

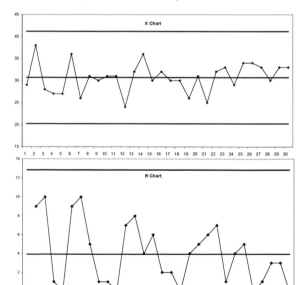

We are tactically tracking the point of sale metric processing time. The central tendency chart shows a very consistent profile.

The variability chart also shows consistency.

With both central tendency and variability consistent, we can prepare our strategic view.

The call processing time SLA is 45 minutes per call. The average is 30.7 minutes per call with a standard deviation of 3.33 minutes. This table shows the call

Strategic View of Call Processing Time	
	Percent Above the SLA of 45 minutes
Predicted	.001%
Actual	0 of 150 or 0.00%

processing time and the histogram below shows our calls are normally distributed. The predicted percent above the SLA of 45 minutes would be .001%.

This strategic view says our center should meet and exceed expectation.

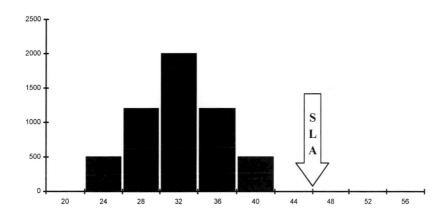

The tactical and strategic views validate our design estimates for the point of sale support area. The central tendency call processing time design estimate was an average of 30 minutes compared to our actual measured average of 30.7 minutes. The variability call processing design estimate was a standard deviation of 3 minutes compared to our actual measured average of 3.33 minutes.

We religiously monitor each metric for change using our tactical view. As long as no changes occur, no strategic studies are required. When the tactical supervisor detects a change, the supervisor must begin the search for the cause and alert the strategic decision-maker to assess the impact. When the cause is determined and the assessment is done, the decision can be made as to what to do.

As time moves on, the tactical supervisor detects a shift in both central tendency and variability of the call processing time. The charts below show those shifts.

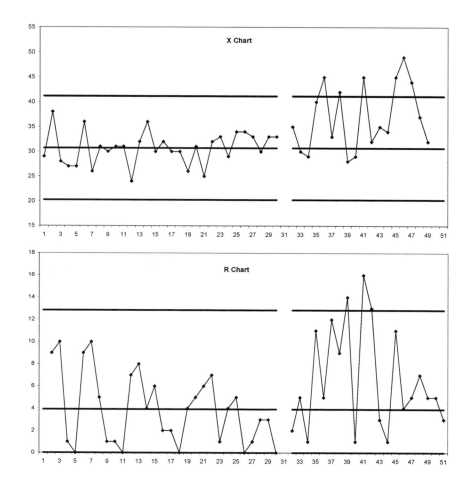

When we start investigating the change, we learn that our software developers have notified us of the release of an update of the point of sale software at the same time the change occurred. This new release of software has many new features that our customers have been asking for. These new features add a new level of complexity to our software.

We realize that the updated point of sales software has caused an increase in the call processing time to explain the new features. The time frame of information after the change will now be compiled to assess the impact on our center. Our call processing time SLA is still 45 minutes per call.

This chart shows where the call processing time is distributed after the new release of software.

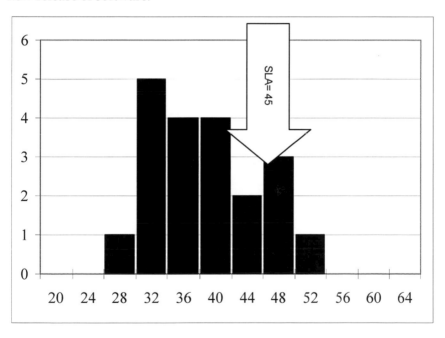

Strategic View of Pickup Time	
	Percent Above the SLA of 45 minutes
Predicted	10.57%
Actual	6 of 60 or 10.0%

The table shows the call processing time with the SLA of 45 minutes per call. The average has increased to 37.1 minutes per call and the standard deviation has also increased to 6.36 minutes. The predicted percent above the SLA of 45 minutes would be 10.57%.

The average call processing time has increased from 30.7 to 37.1. The variability has increased from 3.33 minutes to 6.36 minutes. The call center must be optimized to reflect the higher call processing times.

The following is the information for deciding what to do. First, the new point of sale software release is causing longer call processing times and these increases will be long term. Second, the center is no longer capable of meeting the processing time SLA of 45 minutes and is above the SLA 11% of the time. Third, both central tendency and variability are higher. Fourth, the increases in central tendency and variability are causing the customer wait times to increase.

To bring the wait time back to acceptable levels extra agents must be added, but these additions will have to be hired and will take some time.

Dynamically Retooling the Center to Meet Business Changes

We must now recompute our control limits to reflect the call processing time increase. These charts show that we are consistently (tactical) above the SLA (strategic) ten percent of the time.

These charts show the tactical views for the calls' processing time after the release of the point of sale software. The tactical view values after the new software release are used to calculate the control limits for charts below.

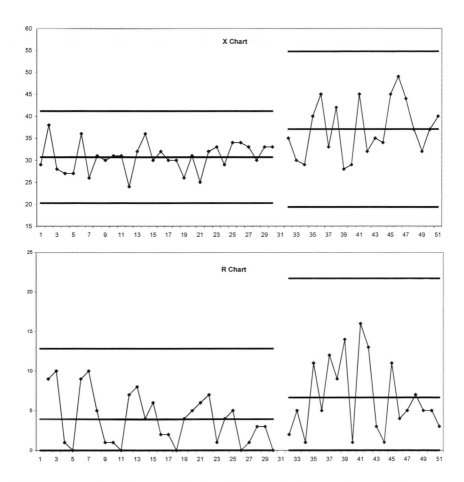

With our tactical views recalculated, the tactical supervisors still have a tool to monitor their role of correct and consistent. If any new changes are detected the revised charts will detect them bringing us back to our change management philosophy.

Chapter Eleven:
Benefits of Effective Metrics

Value to the Customer

Every company values their customers. Customers are the source of their revenue. Many times the company does not act as if they value their customer because they waste their customers' time by making them wait on the phone or computer. If companies paid their customers a cost per minute for each time they made them wait, we might view things very differently. What if the customer charged us $5, or $10, or $20 per hour for waiting? We might rethink some of our strategies. We might find a disconnect between our policy and our strategies. This brings us back to the start of the book where we want to **HAVE IT ALL**.

Results of Running your Call Center with Metrics

Our minimum expectation will start with *superior products and services*. We want to provide services that are as close to our company vision, as our call centers are capable of achieving. We will know where we are not capable so that we can focus our energy and improve. In addition, more productivity, and fewer second and third calls will *reduce unit cost*.

With every call center treated as unique and engineered to its uniqueness, our strategic decision-makers will understand the ability of each call center. With this knowledge they can *detect and repeat improvements, replicate improvements to other areas, fix non-capable call centers, and proactively stop problems before they become a crisis*.

How Will Results Be Achieved?

The total organization works as a team because both strategic and tactical players understand their roles. The tactical supervisors and agents focus their attention on the correct and consistent running of their call center. Running each call center correctly and consistently and to its maximum capability will yield the desired results of better performance and service at lower cost with minimal wait time.

Each call center is run to its maximum design potential. This maximization is due to clearly defined roles and methods, brilliant execution with a process focus, and a clear understanding of the impact. When the call center is run correctly and consistently, the knowledge from the call center's capability study will facilitate optimum performance of each call center.

Quickly responding to change stops problems while they are small. This quick response also allows us to identify the cause of any improvements so that they are continued and replicated into the future.

Let's give a quick recap of the tools that support the call center. Metrics are the glue that ties all the pieces together. In summary, we will get results by using metrics in the following areas:

- Science and engineering
- Walkabout® base camp
- Metric dashboard
- Decision-making team
- Change management proactive decisions

Let's revisit each one briefly.

Science and Engineering

Call center strategic decision-makers must use metrics and science to build and manage state of the art call centers. Understanding call center science is vital to an effective call center.

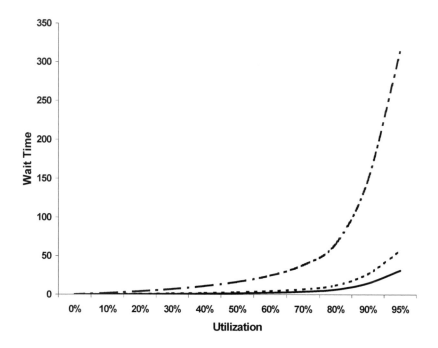

As an example, our *proactive* strategic decision-maker understands that we must manage processing time central tendency, processing time variability, and agent utilization to control wait time and abandonment. Managing through study areas like wait time and abandonment would result in our decisions always being reactionary. Reactionary means crisis management and fire fighting.

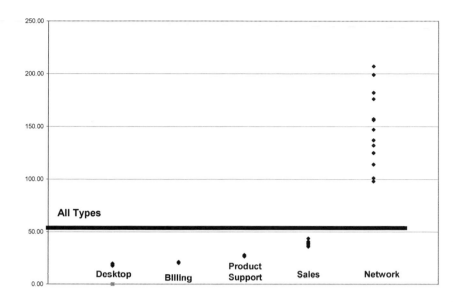

Science and metrics provide the knowledge to proactively manage the center to avoid problems.

Walkabout® Base-camp and the Metric Dashboard

Metric Dashboard

The metric dashboard provides the tools to track the call center base-camp. The dashboard has a dependency, tactical, and strategic view of every metric. The dependency view shows the correctness. The tactical view tracks the metric consistency. The strategic view shows the metric capability.

Chapter Eleven

Correctness

The tactical workforce is dependent on our strategic decision-makers. First, the strategic correctness must be established. Correctness, based on express lanes with clearly defined processes, must be established. The product and process grouping must be correctly calculated. A clearly defined product and a detailed method must be created. The strategic decision-makers must clearly communicate these correct methods. The strategist will provide a Walkabout® diagram of the method. On each metric a target will be provided.

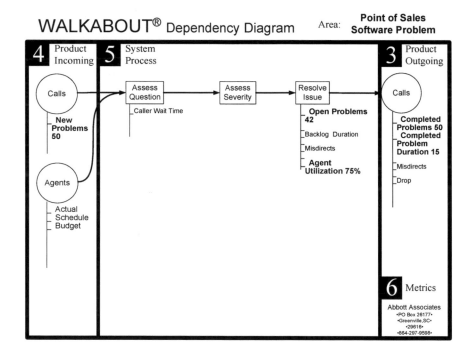

Correct also includes focusing on the processes. The tactical workforce will use the proactive approach of metrics. With a clear understanding of their role, the call center supervisors can focus on the process metrics. These metrics and quick response to change allow a preventive approach to problems.

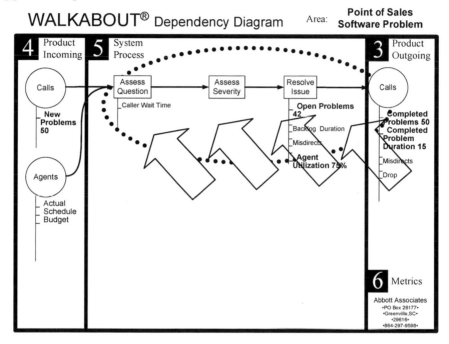

The tactical workforce must brilliantly execute the plan, methods, and the target settings. This brilliant execution should not be confused with perfection. As human beings, we will always strive for perfection but the reality is that it may be outside our grasp. Keep trying to correctly execute the process, but don't worry too much about being absolutely perfect.

Consistency

The second step toward our base-camp requires monitoring each metric for every call center to determine how consistent each product and process metric is. This consistency provides a way of predicting what will be produced time after time. Each call center must have its own consistency established. This consistency is monitored through the use of tactical views.

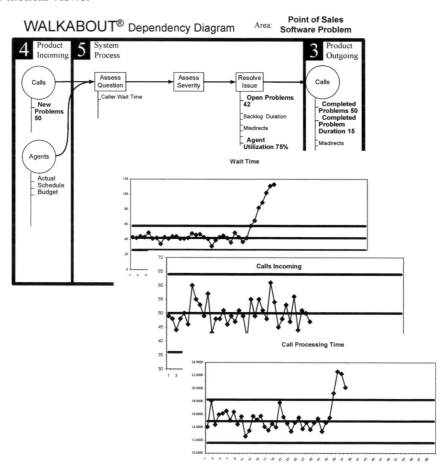

182

Once the tactical product and process issues of correct and consistent are accomplished, our strategic teammates can become active.

Capability

Once the state of correctly and consistently run call centers or processes is reached, the strategic decision-maker is positioned to assess how well the product we make meets the customer's expectation. The strategist uses a strategic view like the one below and understands the importance of central tendency, variability, and distribution on each metric.

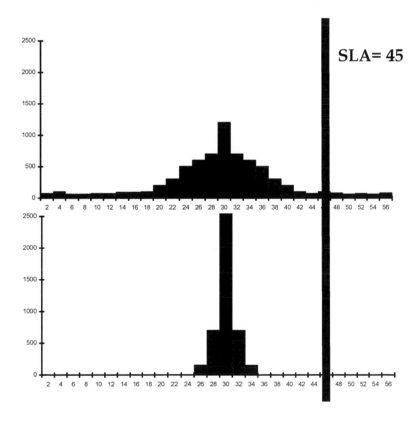

Take special note: correctly and consistently running the provided call center are tactical issues. Capability is a strategic issue. Both the tactician and strategist must work together with brilliance to achieve the best performance from each call center.

The three Cs (correct, consistent, and capable) of the Walkabout® base-camp are the backbone of an effective call center and a profitable business. The metric dashboard gives a comprehensive view of how the center is running.

Decision-making Team

Roles and responsibilities require a clear understanding of division of labor. The following table shows us a summary of the three decision types.

	Executive	Management	Operations
Decisions	Policy	Strategic	Tactical
Terms	Vision	Capability	Control
Tools for Decisions	Market research, Financial reports	Strategic Views from Capability Studies, Service Level Agreements	Tactical View from Control Chart, Control Limits, Targets
Duties	Provide and share the vision	Build a Plan and assess the impact of change	Execute the plan and detect change
Functions	Develop a business vision	Provide the Resources, Time, & Place to resolve plan changes	Detect change, Determine cause

Running your call center is clearly tactical and the job of the tactical decision-maker. These tactical decisions are

- Noting when a change in the process and product metrics has occurred.
- Alerting management when a change has occurred so that the strategic decision-maker can assess the impact of the change on the product or the process.
- Finding the cause of a change.
- Working with the strategic decision maker in deciding what action to take.
- Having the process knowledge to know when and what adjustments are required.

Peak efficiency is dependent on the strategist providing a correct and capable facility. Our tactical work force must count on the strategic players to do their end of the bargain.

Providing the call center facility is clearly strategic and the job of the strategic decision-maker. These strategic decisions are:

- Provide the tools, methods, structure, and technology to meet the policy vision of the executive.
- Assess the impact on the customer or user when a change in the process and product metrics has occurred.
- Dynamically retool the center to meet business changes.

Since strategy and tactics are different, a different metric view for each seems very logical. The tactical view supports the need to detect a change. The strategic view supports the assessment of how well the center is performing, as a function of the customer's needs.

From our discussion of Division of Labor we know the importance of all players executing their role. Metrics are vital to validating the execution of each role and each decision type requires special tools to assess this execution.

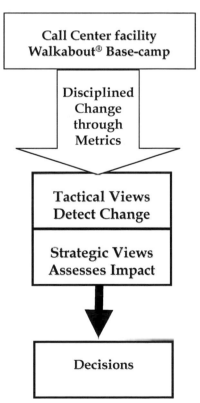

Proactive Decisions through Call Center Change Management

Metrics are our eyes and ears for running and improving the call center. For improvement to occur change must occur. Any time a change occurs, even in the best of circumstances, the result might be negative. Thus we need a change detector and a companion for assessing every change's impact on the call center's capability; this paints the call center's total picture.

Chapter Eleven

Using a change management philosophy provides the means for proactive decisions but only when the change occurs. Between changes our management team can keep their focus on the correct and consistent running of the operation.

Walkabout®

Effective managers walk through their call center and check every area. In Australia, a walkabout is a wandering to see the countryside. In our context, we are wandering in a controlled and disciplined way to assure a correct, consistent, and capable call center. The metric dashboard provides the roadmap, and metrics test the center. The idea of knowledge checklists built from metrics is an essential element for all associates (operations through supervision) to effectively run a process. Effective managers do their daily Walkabouts®. These daily Walkabouts® use the metric dashboard to assess the call center operation.

Effective operations are engineered based on science and metrics—science for direction and metrics for status and verification. Effective operations have a competent workforce that brilliantly executes the engineered plan. We will audit the center with metrics during our Walkabouts®. Optimum decision-making will be based on proper information. Metrics play the key role by providing enough information to make optimal decisions. Metrics support the call center manager.

Effective managers focus their energy on key areas. The key areas are understanding their operation, defining and identifying everyone's roles and responsibilities, and assessing the operation daily for correctness, consistency, and capability. With the Walkabout® metric dashboard as the roadmap, the effective call center manager will rapidly understand their facility inside and out, its operational dependencies, and what the key metrics are. When effective call center managers understand the operation, they define everyone's responsibilities, communicate it to each team member, and have a metric dashboard for checking their daily compliance. This understanding is exactly the role of metrics.

From the start of this book we have worked to provide tools to help all managers be effective. The metric dashboard provides the tools to objectively assess the operation. When a call center manager is doing a daily Walkabout® with a metric dashboard, an effective operation can't be far behind.

The Big Picture

The goal of this book is to run your call centers to their maximum potential all the time. All our efforts are marshaled toward reaching that goal. Running each call center with metrics and science to its maximum potential is vital to an effective operation.

The bigger objective is satisfied customers, stockholders, and a happy call center staff. This objective can be defined as delighting our customer with products that meet or exceed their expectations, while reducing our unit cost, and providing better service to our customers the moment they want it. The three components of this bigger objective are

- Flawless service and performance
- Reducing our cost
- Minimal customer wait time

The performance, cost, and time criteria define the bigger objective.

With metrics, science, and their support tools, reaping the results is a matter of execution and focus. Achieving improved performance, reducing our cost, and reducing wait times is now possible, and will continue.

*We **will** have it all!*

Index

A

Accountability, 11, 184. *See also* strategic role, tactical role, decision making

Alarms, 81, 90
  jump in level, 84
  spread, 88
  too close, 86
  trend, 85

Assessing the center, 174

Average, 46-49

B

Base-camp, 61-62

Bell curve, 80-84, 128-129, 136, 140

Blueprint. *See* Walkabout® Dependency Diagram

C

Call Center
  Types 1-3, 5, 35-41

Call center story, 35

Capability, 32, 65, 75-76, 78, 120-121, 188

Causes, 97-102
  assignable, 100
  common, 100
  special, 100
  tampering, 101

Central tendency, 46, 57, 92-93

Change,
  detecting, 79, 94
  identifying, 90
  investigating, 95-96
  management, 79

Common format, 31

Consistency, 64, 182

Correctness, 63, 180

Customer issues, 110-114, 176

D

Dashboard, 61, 72, 77, 179

Decision making, 25, 68-70, 108-109, 143, 147, 184
  See also accountability, strategic role, tactical role

Dependency diagram. *See* Walkabout® Dependency Diagram

Distribution, 125

Division of labor (second principle of process management), 11

E

Effective manager, 78

Effective operations, 3, 23, 78

Engineering, 165, 177

Express lanes, 18, 169

F

First principle of process
 management, 11

Frequency, 74, 127

G

Goal, 6

Grouping, 148-161
 Associational, 155, 161
 Physical, 160, 162
 Time series, 149, 161

H

Having it all, 14

Histogram, 128

K

Knowledge base, 97-98

M

Management. *See* strategic role
 and Decision making

Manager responsibilities, 4

Metric blueprint. *See* Walk-
 about® Dependency Diagram

Metric measurement, 3

Monitor, 43

N

Normal distribution, 80, 128-132

O

Operations. *See* tactical role

Optimize Your Operation (book),
 33

Out of control. *See* change

P

Pollaczek-Kyntchin, 20, 106

Preparing Call Center Metrics
 (book), 76

Principles of process management. *See* division of labor,
 first principle of process
 management, *and* third
 principle of process management

Process, 65-67

Product, 65-67

Q

Quality, 6-7

Queuing, 14-17, 19-22

R

Range, 50

Report format, 26-29

Reporting flaws, 43

S

Second principle of process management. *See* Division of Labor

Service Level Agreements, 112, 115, 117-118

SLA. *See* Service Level Agreements

Specification limits, 113-114

Spread, 20-22, 49, 124-125

Strategic role, 70
See also accountability, decision making

Strategic terms, 109

Strategy, 109

Subgroup frequency, 74

T

Tactical role, 70
See also accountability, decision making

Tactics, 69

Target, 114

Third principle of process management, 12

V

Variability, 49, 53, 57, 92, 94

W

Walkabout® base-camp. *See* base-camp.

Walkabout® Dependency Diagram, 34-42, 73

Walkabout® Method, 7-9, 186

More titles for enhanced call center design and performance

Preparing Call Center Metrics, $195.00

This companion to *The Executive Guide to Call Center Metrics* is now available directly to readers. Learn the critical metrics and data preparation methods for your call center or help desk.

The Executive Guide to Six Sigma Call Centers, $34.95

Just what executives and managers need to know about call center design and nothing that they don't.

Designing Effective Call Centers, $94.95

The definitive guide to designing call centers and help desks from the ground up.

Order from Amazon.com, your favorite local bookseller, or visit

www.effectivecallcenters.com